MADISON
God's Beautiful Farm

MADISON

God's Beautiful Farm

The E.A. Sutherland Story
by
Ira Gish & Harry Christman

TEACH Services, Inc.
New York

Dedication

We dedicate this book to Seventh-day Adventists throughout all the world, and especially to those who are supremely interested in Christian education, with special emphasis on its reformatory principles as enunciated in the writings of Ellen G. White. Her counsels created the pattern and inspiration for the monumental educational adventure that weaves its way like a golden chord across the span of more than half a century.

2007 08 09 10 11 12 · 5 4 3 2 1

Copyright © 2003 TEACH Services, Inc.
ISBN-13: 978-1-57258-260-X
ISBN-10: 1-57258-260-X
Library of Congress Control Number: 2003106784

Published by
TEACH Services, Inc.
www.TEACHServices.com

Acknowledgments

No one, perhaps, ever sits down and writes a book "all by myself." There are those weeks, months, and sometimes years that a writer disappears from society and hibernates with his typewriter, but even then he knows he is not really writing alone; and if by some lovely plan his book is published, it's going to happen because of a lot of other people. With the present authors, people come in two distinct classes: IDEA and TIME people.

Idea people are those who by their suggestions, books, ideas, or letters have turned us around, shoved us toward writing. At the time of the fiftieth anniversary celebration, the Madison Alumni asked Ira M. Gish to write the life history of Dr. E. A. and Sally Sutherland in the form of a pageant. The pageant was so successful that many suggested he write up the history in book form. With the passing away of Sally Sutherland and later E. A. Sutherland, the manuscript was laid aside and almost forgotten. Years later, through the encouragement and urging of Mable Towery, editor of the *Madison Survey*, Edith Cothran, and Sharon Johnson Holland, Dr. Gish began the work again. This time he asked the cooperation of Elder Harry K. Christman. At the beginning of "the Golden Years of Madison," the two men with their families had lived in the same apartment house on the Madison campus and spent much time together studying the educational program of Dr. Sutherland, admiring together his great success in being guided first by Ellen G. White in person and later in the doctor's careful and willing obedience to the councils of Mrs. White on education.

A host of other idea people molded our thoughts and plans for the book. Among these were Bernard Bowen, Mrs. Agnes Johnson, Elder N. C. Wilson, Dr. M. Hodgen of Loma Linda University. We owe special thanks to the librarians of Madison Academy, Elizabeth Cowdrick and Mary Kate Gifford; to Dr. George Summers, librarian of the Loma Linda University, and his workers in the Heritage Room for their tireless patience in searching through the many letters and papers of Drs. Sutherland and Magan; also to Mable Towery and Elsie Wrinkle.

We especially appreciate the help of Joe E. Sutherland, M.D., only living child of Dr. and Mrs. E. A. Sutherland.

Arthur L. White, of the White Estate, gave us valuable research assistance. Also, Dr. Harry Moyle Tippett helped us tidy up our unsystematic way of writing.

Time people are those who, by giving of their love, encouragement, and time kept us from losing hope and from chalking the whole thing up as a gigantic mistake. With an incredible investment of their understanding, time, faith, and prayers these dear ones pushed, prodded, and pulled us up the long, steep climb. These consisted mostly of our wives who never lost faith in our ability to keep going although we gave up more than once and cried out, "Impossible to go on!"

Every author knows these people are the real writers of any book, and we are personally grateful to them all.

The authors.

Preface

For decades Madison College was synonymous with commitment, sacrifice, and service. I know. For some years I worked very closely with Madison in the Kentucky-Tennessee Conference. Hundreds of young people attended this institution, and here they were challenged with a unique service for the church—self-supporting work. Those who passed through Madison left with a dedication and a commitment to a type of service from which the church benefitted for many years. Madison College and Hospital was the mother institution that, through the Layman Foundation, was responsible for the establishment of many other self-supporting units throughout the southland. These campuses have been a blessing to the work of God. I wish that we had many more such self-supporting schools and hospitals.

When one thinks of Madison College and Hospital one inevitably thinks of Dr. E. A. Sutherland, who played such an important role in building up this institution. I knew Dr. Sutherland during his last years and was impressed with him as a man of God and a man of action. He was an innovator and a man of perseverance. He seemed to thrive on problem solving—and there are many problems in the establishment and development of such an institution as Madison. Dr. Sutherland was a man whom the Lord used to fill a vital role in developing the work of God in the southland.

In their intriguing manuscript, "God's Beautiful Farm," coauthors Ira M. Gish and H. K. Christman have put together the thrilling story of Madison College and Dr. Sutherland, and the beginnings of industrial education among self-supporting Seventh-day Adventist institutions in the southland. This book deals with the traumas and the difficulties faced by the pioneers of this work, with the tests of faith the founders experienced and overcame in God's strength. As veteran author and editor, Harry M. Tippett, said: "Few manuscripts crossing your desk ever had more going for them in documentation, inspiring information, and reader interest."

You will enjoy the story, and I trust that as you read it you will absorb some of the spirit of commitment, dedication, and service that made Madison College an institution long to be remembered, and that figured in the traits of character that made Dr. E. A. Sutherland a truly great leader in God's last-day cause.

R. H. Pierson
Former President
of the General Conference

Contents

Dr. E. A. Sutherland, the founder and builder of the beautiful farm.

CRISIS ON THE CUMBERLAND

On a day in early June 1904 the missionary steamboat *Morning Star* lifted anchor and eased from her moorings at the Nashville landing. The placid Cumberland River ruffled in the dappled shadows of its shoreline verdure as the stern-wheeler pointed her prow upstream.

Edward A. Sutherland, who had recently resigned as president of Emmanuel Missionary College at Berrien Springs, Michigan, stood beside the helmsman, W. O. Palmer, and watched him guide the boat out into the main current with dexterous skill. Sutherland knew that this man had handled riverboats on the streams of the southland for many years.

He turned from his place by the helmsman and considered the passengers on this rather special trip. His gaze rested first on Mother Ellen White,

11

sitting there on the deck with shining eyes lifted to the scene unfolding before them. On her face he saw that look of utter peace that often graced her features while contemplating the lovely things of nature. Sensitive to such beauty himself, he turned for a moment to the river, watching it move between its rocky, wooded banks, rising at times to steep cliffs overhung with sylvan green. He drew a breath of pure delight. Then he thought of the other passengers.

Mother White's two sons had come along on this trip. James Edson White owned the *Morning Star*, and William C. White often accompanied his mother on her itineraries. Her secretary, Clarence Crisler, sat beside Mother White with Sarah McEnterfer and Maggie Hare. Emma White, Edson's wife, had come with them too. Fred Halliday completed the party.

This journey had a twofold purpose: Edson White wanted to find a suitable location for a training school for young black workers in the South while the educators, Edward Sutherland and Percy Magan, intended to look for a place where they might establish a training school for the white young people of that area.

Percy Magan had not yet boarded the *Morning Star*. Edward Sutherland expected him to join the party the next day at Edgefield Junction, some twelve miles above Nashville.

The travelers enjoyed the leisurely cruise, a restful excursion through beautiful sights with enchanting music from the river and the steamboat's machinery.

Suddenly Edward Sutherland realized by the sound of that same machinery that something had gone wrong. "What's the matter with your boat?" he called out to Edson White.

"Another breakdown, I suppose." Edson hurried forward, followed by Sutherland, to examine the boat's running gear. "Looks to me like we'll have to get her towed to shore so we can make repairs," Edson announced. He went off to arrange it.

Edward Sutherland looked about him and saw that they had come to anchor at the head of an island on Neely's Bend, at Larkin Springs.

The men, after assessing the damage, decided that the repairs would not take long. On hearing this news, Mother White suggested that they go ashore and look around. "I'd like to see that farm that we've been talking about. It is close by," she said to Will Palmer.

"Come, Ed," Palmer called, "let's go up and look at the Ferguson-Nelson farm. Mrs. White wants to see it."

"No, indeed," Edward Sutherland backed away. "I've already seen that place, and I'm not the least bit interested in seeing it again."

"But we must go. Mrs. White insists on seeing it."

With reluctance Edward Sutherland, called Ed by his special friends, got off the boat and climbed the bank with the others. He saw that they had indeed come up to the edge of the farm and it looked even worse than he remembered it.

He glanced at Mother White and saw her eyes glistening with enthusiasm. "Ah," she exclaimed, "this looks like a place I have seen in vision. This is the land where God wants Sutherland and Magan to start their training school."

Ed felt a peculiar sinking of his heart, but he

decided to say nothing. They all returned to the boat and found the repairs completed. The party continued upstream to Edgefield Junction where they docked. Here they found Percy T. Magan, the Irishman, waiting for them.

"You promised to be here by noon today, and now it's almost evening," Magan said as he came on board. "I've waited for hours."

"We broke down on the way up," Halliday told him.

"Your old tub is always breaking down. I should have known—"

Halliday interrupted, "We happened to break down right off that Ferguson-Nelson farm, and Mrs. White went over and looked at it."

"Just like your crazy boat to break down where we don't want her to. What happened?" the Irishman asked, overlooking Halliday's comment.

At that moment Will White appeared on deck and walked toward them. "Mother would like to see you two in the cabin," he said to Sutherland and Magan.

They followed Will to the little cabin.

"Well, Brother Magan, I saw your farm today and I walked all around it." Mother White looked up with pleasure in her warm gray eyes. "I'm convinced that God wants you and Ed Sutherland to have that place. It's the kind of place that has been shown me in vision. What do you think of it?"

"I think of it just as little as I can," Magan replied. "It's too big a farm for Ed and me. It's rocky and worn out and barren. It will take more money than we have—"

"Well, I'm sorry," Mother White looked into their faces as she spoke, "because it seems to me that

14

the Lord intends that you shall have that place."

Ed saw that his friend did not want to discuss the matter, so they excused themselves and left the cabin. They went to the stern of the boat and sat there until long after midnight mulling over the events of the day and bemoaning the unfortunate breakdown off the Ferguson-Nelson farm. They had meant to find a quiet place back in the woods and start a small school by themselves. They just couldn't undertake anything big. Why had things taken this turn? At last, after much talk, they decided that they could not and would not be drawn into anything so large, so expensive, and so hopeless. Yet neither of them felt good about the decision, and both of them knew in their deepest hearts that going against Mother White's counsel amounted, somehow, to going against God. A heaviness of heart descended upon them.

The next day the stern-wheeler made its way up to Carthage and anchored there. On the morning of the second day at Carthage Mother White called the two men, Sutherland and Magan, in again. "The Lord wants you to have the Ferguson-Nelson farm and start a training school there," she told them again.

"We can't do it," Ed protested. "We can't call on the denomination to finance such a venture, and we ourselves have insufficient funds to undertake it." Ed marked the undisturbed look on Mother White's face and the uneasy feeling inside him grew until it became a dull ache.

The third morning at Carthage she called them in again and spoke even more urgently about the matter. "I am going to ask Edson to take the *Morning Star* back down to Edgefield Junction. From

15

there we can drive over and have another look at the place."

Sutherland and Magan talked it over and decided not to go to see that farm again. But, when they got to Edgefield Junction, Mother White asked Will Palmer to drive her over to the farm. A few hours later she came back aboard the boat and reported that she had talked to the Fergusons, the owners, who lived on the property. She had told them that her group wanted that land in order to start a school for Christian workers. Again she urged Sutherland and Magan to buy the property.

"We understand," Ed began, "that the price of this place is between twelve and thirteen thousand dollars. This amount is more than double what we intend to pay for land. On no account can we invest more than five thousand dollars." He sat down by Mother White and spoke in earnest tones. "Mother White, we are determined to go no farther than our means will allow. Our idea is to take a small place back in the hills where we can make friends with our neighbors and help them and build slowly."

Ellen White looked into their faces and smiled that gentle smile of hers. "I am afraid you will make your plans too small and set your aim too low. If you will follow the counsel of the Lord, He will set your feet in a large place and provide the money to pay for it." She stood up and pointed an admonishing finger. "Are you two men to bury your talent in the ground? Has the Lord given you all these years of experience and the ability to train others for His work that you might tell Him, 'Lord, we knew thee that thou art a hard man . . . and we were afraid and went and hid thy talent in the earth'?"

16

Edward Sutherland felt a wave of distress sweep over him. "No, no, Mother White," he said. "We will work for the Lord. We want to do His will, but we don't have the twelve or twenty or forty thousand dollars it will take to start a school on that place."

The following day Sutherland and Magan hired a horse and buggy. They drove in another direction from the Ferguson-Nelson land. They went to look at another farm. But, drawn by a mixture of emotion and curiosity which they did not stop to analyze, in the afternoon they found themselves back at the Ferguson-Nelson farm. They knew that they were not the only ones looking over this property. Ed had seen Will Palmer drive off with Mother White earlier. Edson and Sarah McEnterfer had gone with them.

Now the two men, Sutherland and Magan, stood looking at the limestone rocks sticking up through the pasture grass, and the ledges laid bare in the lean fields and cropping out of crests and slopes of the barren hills.

They walked over to a pile of stones near the old plantation barn and sat down on a rock. Across the red-gulleyed, water-washed, ridged stretch of the south field they saw acres of stony ground where once the cabins of six-hundred blacks used to be, for this farm had once been a slave-trader's headquarters.

Ed could not imagine a more forbidding and desolate prospect for a school. "Percy," he said as he stretched his hand out toward the dreary fields, "it's the roughest, weediest, most miserable thing I've ever seen. It does me up and makes me sick, the whole thought of it."

17

"I know, Ed, I feel the same; but Sarah McEnterfer says that the farm Mother White selected for the Cooranbong School in Australia was pronounced worthless by the leaders there."

"Well, it can't have been as bad as this," Ed said. "Look at that loathesome old barn and those stinking hogpens up against the parlor windows of the plantation house."

They sat for a few minutes, sunk in a morass of self-pity and discouragement. Finally Ed spoke again. "That Australian school is really flourishing now, I guess."

"Yes, Mother White told them not to reject the Lord's counsel, but give Him a chance to work."

Ed recalled with great clarity similar words spoken to him yesterday. He felt worse every minute, but still he resisted. He turned searching eyes on Percy. "I do believe that you started Mother White on this tangent about the Ferguson-Nelson property." Then, seeing the incredulous look on Percy's face, he burst into tears. "Oh, I wish we had some honorable and Christian way to get out of the whole thing without showing lack of faith in the testimonies from the Lord's messenger."

Broken, utterly discouraged, the men knelt and poured out their hearts to God. Then, calmed and resolute, they decided to take a short option on the farm. They would step out by faith alone and obey the counsel given them by God through Mother White. Then they went back to tell her of their decision. She did not seem surprised, but commended their action with kind words.

The next morning the two men drove to the farm again. They knelt among the rocks by the old plantation barn, and again they begged the Lord to show them His will and to strengthen them to be obedient. Appalled at the risks they were incurring, tormented by doubts, they wrestled with the Lord in an agony of supplication.

They faced an initial outlay of between thirteen and fifteen thousand dollars for the place with the meager facilities it offered. They had not half the money to pay for the bare, rocky, miserable land, to say nothing of building and equipping a training school. They prayed to the Almighty for help. And courage flowed into them in such abundant measure that at no future time did they doubt that God had led them in this venture, and that He would take charge and direct all that concerned the whole undertaking.

They had passed through their Gethsemane. They had wrestled all day with the problem. Now twilight had begun to throw a merciful mantle over the stark and barren landscape. The birds hushed their singing and sought their nests. Squirrels scampered into the old trees, and the straggly flowering plants looked like pale exclamation points against the dark shadows of night.

Percy Magan spoke up, "Ed, we are in it—in it voluntarily. Mrs. White is with us. God is leading us. He will show us the way."

Suddenly, with a strong and joyful voice, Ed began singing "Faith of our fathers living still—" Percy joined him, and the praises to God rang out over that desolate and worn-out farm. Perhaps in that moment of triumphant faith, the angels of God came down and claimed this farm for their own.

The song ended, and the stillness of night fell round them. The lonely hills shut them in and a heaven of stars arched above them. A solemn sense of the Divine Presence enfolded them, and they began singing again:

> "After storm the rainbow shineth,
> Promise writ in light above;
> Even so, across our sorrow
> Shines the rainbow of His love."

The usual buoyancy of the bubbling Irishman appeared. "Ed," Percy chose every word with care, "here we are at the parting of the ways. If we had taken the position that what Mother White says is not of the Lord, then we would not have been ready to accept anything the Lord tells her unless it conforms to our opinions."

"There's no other way," Ed replied, "if we want to go on and have the assurance that God is with us. Let's hurry back to Nashville and tell Mother White that we will buy the Ferguson-Nelson farm."

When they told her of their final decision, she showed great pleasure. "I'll do anything to help you," she told them. "Go out and tell your story to the people, and they will help you. I will recommend your work and write an article about it in our church paper. I'll come on your board if you wish." (This was the only time in her life that she agreed to become a member of the board of trustees of any institution.)

Edward Sutherland and Percy Magan had staked their future, their very lives on the counsel God had given to Mother White. They determined that regardless of price, toil and/or hardships they would stand by the project and put it through under God to a successful finish.

"Christ's most favorite theme was the paternal character and abundant love of God."—*Testimonies to Ministers*, p. 192.

BATTLE OF THE ANGELS

When Edward Sutherland and Percy Magan made their decision to follow the counsel of God in regard to the Ferguson-Nelson property, their attitude toward the place altered. Ed began to envision it as it could become with God's blessing resting upon it. He began to see its potential and to plan for it. Percy shared his growing enthusiasm. They acted at once. Ed went north to Berrien Springs to raise money for the undertaking, while Percy took the money they had available and went out to make a payment to extend the option.

Nashville, that summer evening in late June 1904, flamed with beauty and color. Percy Magan walked through the pleasant streets, breathing in the delightful perfume from the rose gardens on the avenues. He felt in tune with nature and with his heavenly Father. He sang softly to himself as he walked. Percy Magan had reason to sing. He was on his way to the home of the Fergusons, owners of the 400-acre tract of land near Nashville that he and Edward Sutherland were going to buy and use for a training school. He had the money in his pocket to make a token payment to hold the option on the property until Ed could return with more money.

Percy recounted in his mind God's leading in this whole sequence of events. He recalled Mother White's assurance that the Lord had shown her that this neglected, barren farm would, under His blessing, become a "great center of educational work, a spectacle to the world, to angels, and to men." She had called it a "beautiful farm." Percy knew that God must have chosen the spot Himself. Certainly no man would have chosen it.

Both Edward Sutherland and Percy Magan had discussed the price of the place with the owners, and they had agreed to sell it for a certain stated amount. Percy felt sure that the deal was as good as made. He knocked on the Ferguson door with confidence.

Mr. Ferguson threw open the door. "Well, professor, I'm afraid all our time has been spent for nothing. Miz Sallie will not sell. I'm ashamed, but I can't help it."

"What's the matter with Miz Sallie?" Percy asked.

"I hate to tell you," the man looked down at his feet, "but she sez that a Yankee shall never own this place."

"Let me see her." Percy stepped inside the room. "We made a bargain with you people, and my friend has already gone north to get the purchase money. You don't want to lay yourselves liable for a lawsuit, do you?"

"I don't think you'd better see her," the husband warned. When Miz Sallie gets in a tantrum, she acts like the very devil."

"Maybe so, but I've talked more than once to women who acted like the devil," Percy assured him.

Mr. Ferguson led Percy into the south parlor and told him to wait there. In a few moments he came back into the room, a great tall fellow, with his wife, taller than he, right behind him. If Percy could have conjured up in his mind an image of Jezebel, she stood before him now in this impressive woman, he thought.

"Miz Sallie," the husband began, "I want to introduce you to Professor Magan."

She turned on her husband, stamped her foot, and hissed, "You get outta this room, sir." He hastened away. Then she turned to Percy. "And now, sir, what do you want?"

"Miz Sallie," he spoke gently, "if you'll sit down and be quiet a moment, I'll talk to you."

She flopped into a chair.

"Now," he said, "your husband tells me that you don't want to sell the place. You have put us in a hard position, because you have agreed to sell. My friend has gone north—"

"I'll never sell to a—a—a Yankee."

Percy softened his voice even more. "Miz Sallie, were you ever a Christian?" He didn't know why he had asked her that question. The words had just come to him.

He saw her eyes fill with tears. She burst into sobbing and said, "Oh, I used to be. My father was a Methodist minister, and he brought me up to be a Christian woman, but it seems as though the very devil has gotten into me."

"Your husband told me that," Percy said. "Now listen to me, Miz Sallie, if the Lord doesn't want us to have this place, we don't want it. Let's kneel right now and ask the Lord to show us whether this thing is right."

Miz Sallie cried and sobbed as though her heart had broken, and they got down on their knees and prayed. Percy prayed, "Oh Lord, take the devil out of Miz Sallie."

She prayed, "Oh Lord, I know there's a devil in me, and I want you to cast him out."

When they rose from their knees, Percy saw that her face had softened and she seemed more relaxed. "You draw up that contract," she told him, "and I'll sign it."

Percy went to work on the contract at once, and after a little while sweet and smiling she came back into the parlor and invited him to have dinner with them. After dinner, they chatted for a few minutes; then she went upstairs while Percy went back to the parlor to finish the contract. At last he called out, "Mr. Ferguson, it's all ready. Now we can sign up."

The man went upstairs, and Percy waited for half an hour. He could feel the day growing dark; the atmosphere became oppressive. Finally Mr. Ferguson returned. "Professor," he said, "it's all off again. She's acting like the devil's in her again. Her daughters are up there beseeching her, but it's no use.

"Well," Percy said, "get her down here again."

"No, it's no use."

24

"Yes, it is some use," Percy said, "because we are going to have this farm."

"How can you be sure of that?"

"You wouldn't understand if I told you, but I know it. Get her down here."

About half an hour later she came down, and they sat on the porch and talked back and forth. She told Percy how she hated the Yankees.

The good mood induced by their prayers had vanished. She seemed to know that something had touched her when they prayed, but now the perverse spirit had entered her mind again. She veered back and forth between wanting to sell and not wanting to sell.

"I will keep coming back," Magan told her, "until we get the farm." He had an idea that one purpose of Miz Sallie's tantrums was to raise the price.

That night he telegraphed his friend Edward Sutherland, telling him he'd better come down again. They would evidently have to pay more. He asked him to bring Mother Druillard with him. He insisted they both ought to come.

While waiting for them, Percy Magan held a conference with Miz Sallie every day on the Ferguson porch. Finally, in a brief cooperative mood, she made Magan an offer which upped the price about $700.00. He got a verbal option from her for that price. The option was to hold until the following Wednesday—only a verbal option. Miz Sallie would sign nothing.

When Edward Sutherland received the telegram, he went directly to the home of Mrs. W. H. Druillard at Berrien Springs. Mrs. Druillard was Ed's aunt and affectionately called by all Mother

D. She had one of the shrewdest financial heads in the denomination. She had acted as treasurer and financier in several places, including a post in Africa; and she managed for all of her life to be a capitalist and also the Lord's almoner, with one of the most generous of hearts united with her cool head. She was now treasurer of Emmanuel Missionary College.

Edward Sutherland asked Mother D to put up the purchase price for the Ferguson-Nelson Farm.

Mother D questioned him on all aspects of the proposition. "It looks unstable and risky to me," she said. "How is it that you've changed your idea of buying a small farm? Now here you come with a $12,000 proposition."

"That's just the start, Mother D," Ed explained. "The school will need to be equipped and the farm stocked with machinery and tools."

"What were you boys thinking of," Mother D interrupted, "to involve yourselves in a deal so far beyond your resources?"

"We were thinking just what you think." Ed gave her a twisted grin. "And we intended to keep on thinking that way, but God put a bit in our mouths and turned us around." He explained all that had happened.

"Ed, it's harebrained. I'll not give you the money. I can't go into such a thing."

Ed felt a strange determination surge up within Him. "Well, then," he said, "I'll go and get the money from someone else." He arose and reached for his hat. "Magan and I are going to obey the Lord."

He opened the door and walked out; but she called him back. "Look, Ed," she laid her hand on

26

his arm. "I'll go down with you and look this thing over."

They took the train for Nashville. At the station waiting for them they found Elder Butler, Elder Haskell and his wife, Mother White, Sarah McEnterfer, C. C. Crisler, and Percy Magan.

Magan grabbed Sutherland's hand. "Ed, the jig is up. The old lady has broken her contract. She wants a thousand dollars more."

"Ha!" Mother D exclaimed. "I'm glad we're not going to take it."

Mother White's eyes sparkled. "Glad!" her clear voice rang out. "Glad! Do you think I'd let the devil beat me out of a place for a thousand dollars? Pay the extra thousand. It's cheap enough. This is the place the Lord said you should have."

Then she turned to Mother D. "Nell, you think that you are almost old enough to retire, but if you will cast in your lot with this work, if you will look after these boys and guide them and support them in what the Lord wants them to do, then the Lord will renew your youth and you will do more in the future than you have ever done in the past."

The whole party drove to the old frame house, headquarters of the Southern Publishing Association, where Mother White was staying. While the others prayed, Magan, Sutherland, and Mother D drove the nine miles to the farm to call on the Fergusons.

They were ushered into the parlor and seated.

"Do you want the place?" Miz Sallie said as she came into the parlor.

"Of course we want it," Magan told her. "We have decided to take up that option."

She shook her head, "Don't know whether I'll

sign or not, but if I were in Nashville, I might."

Magan took her by the arm and put her and her husband in the buggy that they had driven out in. They all returned to Nashville.

Miz Sallie's demon of perversity still swung her round and round. She wanted to sell. She didn't. She would and she wouldn't. They drove straight to a notary's office.

Under Tennessee law a married woman can break her word and be free of any obligation. If a deed or contract of sale is signed by both husband and wife, the woman must go into a room with the notary with none of her kin present and sign an oath saying she has not been coerced. She stamped her foot. "I'll never sign that! I'm not doing this thing freely." She bit her lip and turned pale. "The—the—Yankee! The—the—Yankee!" she kept muttering under her breath.

Her husband came into the room. "Oh, Sallie," he shook his fist, "do quit that!"

"They've got to pay me in gold," she screamed.

"No," he said, "their check is as good as gold."

Finally she turned to the notary, "I subscribe to that oath, sir. Give me the pen." She took the pen and scribbled her name.

Magan handed her a check for the down payment, $5000.00, most of it borrowed money. Then the two young educators took the papers and got out of the office.

They went at once to see Mother White and told her, "Mother White, we have the place."

"Well, Brother Sutherland," she gave them her warmest smile, "you boys will never know how many angels worked to help you get it."

Percy Magan felt a thrill of joy run through him.

Like Daniel, he had entreated the Lord, and the angels had fought for him even as they fought with the Prince of Persia.

Edward Sutherland in that fall of 1904 faced the greatest challenge of his life—the commitment to establish, equip, and bring to success on the barren acres of the Ferguson-Nelson farm a training school to meet the needs of the South. He had reached his thirty-ninth year, and, with Percy Magan four years younger, he had passed the acid test of faith required to step out on an unconditional belief in the counsel of Mother Ellen White.

"We do not have faith," he told his friend Percy, "unless we do believe in something that does seem out of reach of the human mind."

"And this proposition is just such a thing." Percy Magan stood beside him. They had come out again to look at the land with eyes made keen by ownership and responsibility.

Mother Druillard was with them. She had invested money in that unpromising land. Now she stood with the wind tossing her red hair in which the gray had begun to show. Ed looked at Mother D. How young she looked for sixty! Red-headed people don't show their age as do others, he thought. He watched her as she stretched an eloquent hand over the forbidding acres and said, "The trees, the hills, and the sky look good. But this farm is like a desert. See how the hogs have torn out the grass by the roots and made even the dooryard a desolation." She stood silent for a moment and then suddenly turned to the two men. "You know what made me willing for this deal to go through?" Without waiting for a reply, she hurried on, her face lit with a radiance that shone from within. "Sister White told me that if I will give my time, my talent, and my means to help establish the school here, God will give me the privilege of doing so, and I shall live to see the work a success."

Ed spoke up. "To believe things that are perfectly reasonable requires no faith." His calculating scrutiny took in the whole 400 acres of their newly acquired land. "I don't know why we shouldn't expect God to work miracles now just as He did when He turned water to wine and opened the Red Sea."

> **"All right inventions and improvements have their source in Him who is wonderful in counsel and excellent in working."**—
> *Counsels to Teachers*, p. 277.

TRAILBLAZING

Edward A. Sutherland had come to this venture of beginning a new training school with years of experience in education. Godly parents had begotten him and instilled in him the "fear and admonition of the Lord," and a childhood and youth of commitment to God lay in his background.

His father, Joseph Sutherland, educated in Glascow to be a teacher of Greek and Latin, had migrated with his parents to Canada and then to Wisconsin, where they settled on a farm near the Rankin family. The Rankins had eight red-headed daughters. Joseph Sutherland married Mary Rankin. Shortly after their marriage the young couple embraced the Seventh-day Adventist message and became ardent adherents of the faith.

In 1865 Joseph and Mary Sutherland left their Wisconsin home and began a journey to Otronto,

Iowa. They were expecting their first child and hoped to reach their journey's end before the baby came; but on their way, at Prairie du Chien, in Crawford County, on the freezing morning of March 3, 1865, while their caravan crossed the Mississippi River, Edward Alexander was born.

From his father, Joseph, young Edward inherited his forthright honesty and business ability, combined with a rare talent for making friends and holding them. From his mother, Mary, he inherited his literary ability and his gift for skillful management. Both parents threw around him a security born of an active faith in God.

All through his childhood Edward felt the refining influence of song and prayer. Morning and evening worship fixed the boundaries of his days. His mother's songs of praise and his father's strong prayers built a wall of assurance around him and later around Lydia, his sister. They knew the peace of a well-ordered home.

Edward learned early the value of labor and the patience taught by life on a farm with its multitude of responsibilities and activities. He and Lydia herded cows for a penny a day. When the summer ended, he had amassed the sum of thirty-five cents. The long winter presented many temptations to spend his money, but he resisted them, and spring found his small hoard intact.

His father suggested that they invest the thirty-five cents in onion sets, and Edward helped plant them. He tended the onions all summer, harvested them in the fall, sold the dry onions and realized quite a fortune from his first business venture. Through this experience he learned lessons of patience, industry, and frugality.

About this time a new possibility opened before him. Skunks had become so prolific and destructive that the county offered a bounty for them. Thinking to earn some quick and easy money, Edward applied himself with skill and energy. He managed to corner his first skunk. Now he had only to swing his club and kill the skunk; but the skunk went into action first. The animal got away, but the boy didn't.

Choking and terrified he ran to his mother, who barred him from the house, took him out to the pasture, stripped and scrubbed him and buried his clothes in the ground. His gain from this new venture was other than financial, but of equal value. Edward Sutherland learned how to deal with skunks and he did not forget. "When you meet a skunk, leave him alone. If you don't, you will soon smell just like one."

Ed graduated from the Otronto High School at the age of nineteen. The following school year he taught a neighboring country school, riding back and forth on his pony, Mouse. That year of teaching, 1884-85, made him realize how much more he must learn in order to be a trained and successful teacher of children and youth. He determined to go to college.

One morning at breakfast he announced, "I want to go to college. I want to go to Battle Creek."

"You've already got your education, Son," his father answered. "All you have to do is earn enough money to buy a good piece of land so you can develop a nice farm." Father seemed to consider the matter closed.

"But I don't want to be a farmer. I want to be a teacher." Young Edward had all the stubborn per-

33

sistence of both the Sutherlands and the Rankins. He stood his ground.

"You know there is no money for going to college," Father said.

Edward considered this problem for a few minutes. "Then I will sell Mouse. That will give me enough money to get to Battle Creek, and I'll find a way to get what I want."

Edward did sell Mouse, although it cost him anguish to part with the beloved pony. That fall of 1885 he went to Battle Creek. But he did not go to college. His aunts, Ida Rankin, preceptress in the girl's dormitory at Battle Creek College, and Effie, matron in charge of food services, took Edward in that first year; he spent all his time studying grammar and rhetoric under the private tutelage of Professor Goodloe H. Bell. Even though letters from home informed him of his entire family's disapproval, he carried through on his program of English study. The following year he enrolled in Battle Creek College.

At the end of his first college year, Edward decided to return home and spend the summer of 1887 helping his father on the farm. His muscles were soft and the work was hard. So was his father.

Harvest and threshing time came on. A conveyor carried the straw from the threshing machine to the stack, where a man handled it with a pitchfork. All the men on the crew regarded that job as the hardest. Father Joseph put Edward on that job. The men observed his blistered hands and protested. His mother cried, but the father insisted, "It will do him good," he said. "I want to find out what that boy is made of."

He found out. Edward worked and sang and

prayed his way through that threshing season as "straw-monkey" without complaint.

The next summer Edward colporteured to earn money for school. While selling books, he stayed at the home of Mrs. Josephine Gotzian in the fashionable Dayton Bluff section of St. Paul, Minnesota. The previous year the wealthy Mrs. Gotzian had gone to Battle Creek Sanitarium as a patient and had accepted the Adventist faith. Other young men had stayed at the Gotzian home, and because they did not find the food to their liking, they had a most unpleasant time there. Edward resolved that if it were possible, he would please this good lady. He went out of his way to do services for her. He groomed her horse and did errands about the place for his board and room. Evenings and Sundays he took her riding through the park in a carriage drawn by her beautiful horse, Major. Remembering his own beloved Mouse, Edward took special care of Major.

The young man could not foresee how this unique friendship with Mrs. Gotzian would affect his future. So simple and unimportant do the beginnings of God's wonders sometimes appear to human eyes.

In that year of 1888 God kindled a great light at the Minneapolis Conference through the message of righteousness by faith. That light changed Edward's life and motivated his plans and actions for his remaining years.

In the fall of 1888 when Edward returned to Battle Creek College for his third year, he acquired a new friend, Percy T. Magan, an Irish lad. A friendship sprang up between these two young men not unlike that between Jonathan and David.

Their personalities and capabilities complemented each other and led to a combination of their efforts unparalleled in the Seventh-day Adventist denominational work.

No chance circumstance placed Edward Sutherland and Percy Magan directly under Mother Ellen White's influence in the late autumn of 1888, when she herself was filled to overflowing with joy and interest in the message of righteousness by faith, which she declared to be "the third angels' message in verity." She invited Percy to come and live in her home. And that winter Edward often visited his friend. They studied the deep truths of the three angels' messages, the investigative judgment, the sanctuary and the atonement, all in the glorious new light of the 1888 message. From intimate contact with Mother White they learned to value the marvelous gift to the remnant church that God had bestowed on this gentle woman.

They marked the self-sacrificing life she lived and the simple appointments of home. They experienced the aura of peace and joy that filled that humble home. They came to know the standards Ellen White upheld and the selfless concern she had for the growing work. They both called her Mother White, a title of endearment that they used for the rest of their lives. The conviction that the revelations to Mother White came from God struck deep into the hearts and minds of both young men and shaped all their future action.

Although Percy lacked four years of Edward's age, the younger man had a profound influence on the older. Edward soon discovered that Percy enjoyed a religious experience that he himself did not know. Percy had yielded the inner citadel of his life to God and had accepted righteousness by faith in Jesus without question or reservation.

"Percy, tell me how you can claim the promises with such complete faith," Edward said during one of their long talks on spiritual matters. "Of course I believe the Bible and all that, but I still find doubts and fears in my heart sometimes. I guess my faith just hasn't grown enough."

Percy looked at him with deep affection. "Maybe it will help to remember how big God is, how long He has lived, and the resources He has for fulfilling those promises."

Little by little, Percy led Edward into a full acceptance of the righteousness of Christ and complete dependence on the great and precious promises. Every visit Edward made to Mother White's home and every conversation with her strengthened the new experience until both he and Percy were "rooted and grounded" in the saving doctrines of Jesus Christ.

And Percy taught Edward about recreation too. Edward noticed that Percy got his exercise by doing useful and profitable work. Percy had entered the college bakery and soon became head baker. He worked in the kitchen and learned to cook. He worked in the machine shop and became proficient with tools. Edward got his recreation playing football and baseball.

One day Edward laid hold on Percy's firm arm. "We need another man on our baseball team, a man with this kind of muscle, Percy."

"Not interested." Percy turned away.

"But why? Do you think we should work all the time?"

"Let's say that I can't regard any activity as recreation suitable for me unless it confers benefit on someone."

"Surely vigorous exercise is healthful and necessary for the body," Edward insisted.

"Yes, exercise is good and necessary; but to my way of thinking, such exercise can be gotten in profitable ways. True recreation brings blessing to others."

Edward thought long and deeply over his friend's words and example. In time he came to believe as Percy did about recreation. So passed another milestone on his march toward greatness.

A certain young lady from Iowa, Sally V. Bralliar, attended Battle Creek College and some of the same classes that Edward did. Edward found her to be very talented, educated in German and Latin, an artist, and a domestic science major. He also found that she had a sterling character. Besides this Edward learned that they both had the same goals, one of which was to teach. He found her altogether attractive; and when their eyes met across the classroom a delightful feeling swept over him and sparks of electricity seemed to chase up and down his spine. Although the rules of the college restricted association between men and women students, Edward found a way to let Sally know that she pleased him very much. As always love found a way; and before graduation these two had promised to share their lives and love with each other. The faculty approved and gave its blessing.

In June 1890 the couple graduated from Battle Creek College. Edward received his ministerial license and faced the future with confidence and enthusiasm. He went to be tent master for Elder R.

Sally and Edward Sutherland shortly after their marriage.

C. Porter's effort in Winnepage City, Minnesota, while Sally went home to prepare for her wedding. They were married in August and began a long and useful career. The influence of this dedicated couple would reach round the world.

After their wedding Edward took his bride to Minneapolis, Minnesota. He took over the principal's position at the academy that fall, replacing C. A. Lewis, who had been called to Union College in Lincoln, Nebraska.

The year went well. Sally and Edward Sutherland grew to understand each other and discovered many qualities in one another that deepened their affection and welded them into a single instrument for God's use.

One morning in the spring Edward came home from his classes unexpectedly. "What's wrong? Why are you home at this hour of the day?" Sally asked as he came into the house.

Edward took off his coat and took his lovely Sally in his arms. "I almost hate to tell you. You have made such a snug little home for us here; but a man from Union College has come, and they want us to go to Union next year. You are to head the art department, and I am to head the history department."

"Of course we will go!" Sally looked into his eyes with that searching look that always made Edward feel that she could read his soul.

"Well, I told the man that I would come home and pray with you about it and we would decide. He wants to know right away."

They knelt together as they did morning and evening and at other special times when they needed to commune with God.

They decided to go.

"Now as never before we need to understand the true science of education. If we fail to understand this, we shall never have a place in the kingdom of God. 'This is life eternal, that they may know thee, the only true God and Jesus Christ whom thou hast sent.' If this is the price of heaven, shall not our education be conducted on these lines."—Christian Educator, August 1897, p. 22. Quoted in the *Journal of True Education*, February 1947.

YEARS OF DECISION

Edward's friend, Percy Magan, had stayed on at Battle Creek College. His education had been interrupted, however, by an urgent need for his services as a history teacher. While Edward had wrestled with the problems of his first year as academy principal, Percy delved deep in preparation for his history classes. He studied beyond the requirements of his course. Especially he studied Mother White's writings on educational reform and related subjects. When the first year of his college teaching ended, he stood committed to certain basic principles of reform that would enlist him as their champion for the remainder of his life.

After Edward's first year as academy principal in Minneapolis, the Sutherlands moved to Union College and settled into their new home there. Then they left for Harbor Springs, Michigan, to attend the first general educational convention of the Seventh-day Adventist Church. The effects of the Minneapolis Conference of 1888 and its message of righteousness by faith had made a mighty impact; yet the reaction rose slowly, and a feeling of change charged the air when one hundred teachers gathered for this six weeks of study.

Edward met and renewed his friendship with Percy Magan there. "Percy," he said when the first hearty greetings were over, "I hear there's wonderful fishing around Harbor Springs. Let's take a day off and go fishing." Edward thought no treat more delicious than a pan of fresh-caught fish fried in butter.

"Fishing has lost its lure for me," Percy said, and then Edward saw the mischievous twinkle in his eye. Percy explained that he had become a vegetarian and had no interest in catching fish or any other animal for food. "You know, Mother White has received light on the kind of diet we should have."

So persuasive were Percy's arguments and so firmly backed by inspired reasoning that the young Sutherlands became vegetarians from that day forward.

Now the two men began discussing other important matters. Both Percy and Edward had a strong sense of advancing into increasing light. The messages Mother White brought to the young church called for expansion into strange new areas by paths untried. And now a hundred of the foremost educators of the church had convened to consider the basic principles of the new education which Mother White seemed to think so important.

"How do you feel about this idea of Mother

White that our schools should be located in rural areas?" Edward asked Percy the first chance he had when they were able to talk alone.

Percy thought for a moment. "Of course you know I agree." He gave his friend that charming Irish smile. "The whole thing goes together—country location, plenty of fertile land, teachers and students working together and making a successful job of supporting themselves. Sounds good to me."

"That's one of the basic principles, isn't it?" Edward said thoughtfully.

"Yes, but it's not the first basic principle. The first one is that a knowledge of God is the essential education, that His Word should be the principle textbook, with the book of nature running a close second."

Edward recalled that Mother White had been advocating such a program of education for some time, even before the founding of Battle Creek College. He wondered why these messages which the church had been so slow to follow had come to seem of urgent importance now. Could it be that the Minneapolis message of righteousness by faith had opened enough hearts and minds that maybe God would do something important at this convention for the educators?

"Percy, I'd like to go south and begin work in one of the Southern States. Mother White has talked so much about the needs of the South. Maybe we should go there," Edward announced.

"If we are willing, I think God will open the way for us to work where He needs us most," Percy answered.

As the basic principles of education were discussed at that convention in 1891, Edward found himself in full sympathy with them all and felt a great eagerness to press forward along these lines of service. He would talk to Mother White about it. Then he realized that Mother White wouldn't be around to talk to. She had determined to go to Australia. For seventeen years she had been trying to get the brethren to move Battle Creek College to a country location, but they had done nothing. Although she still maintained tender ties of affection with these same brethren, she had felt led of God to make the move to Australia, where she hoped a school could be established and carried forward according to God's plan.

One evening near the close of the convention Edward hurried to the room where he and Sally were staying. "Sally, what do you think has happened now?"

"I couldn't guess." She smiled as though she already knew that his news was good.

"We aren't going to teach at Union College this fall after all. The General Conference has called us back to Battle Creek College."

"What will we teach?"

"I'm to teach history, and you are to head the art department and teach German."

Sally sat down in the nearest chair. "It's a good thing we didn't get all our things unpacked there in College View." She sighed but smiled up at her husband.

The young Sutherlands went back to Union College to pack their few belongings and returned to Battle Creek College. They both counted it an honor to be on the faculty of their beloved alma mater.

Just before school opened, the president informed Edward that he would teach, not history as he had planned, but Bible. "We didn't expect this upset, Edward, but we have to make the best of it. I'm sure you understand."

So Edward took up his duties as Professor Sutherland in the denomination's most important college. He had no textbook, no syllabus, not even an outline. He taught Old Testament History and acted as preceptor of the men's hall.

While his newly espoused vegetarian diet composed only a minor part of his convictions on education and life, yet this matter posed the first serious problem in his new role as a college teacher.

He reasoned that Old Testament History should begin with Genesis. Bravely he led his class into the first chapters of Genesis, where they discovered, and discussed at length, the diet God gave man in his perfect, Edenic state. The students questioned, "Is there any reason why this same kind of diet should not be used now?"

They studied into the ninth chapter of Genesis. There they found that the first use of flesh food was permitted only after the earth had been devastated by the Flood. More questions arose.

The young Bible professor did not hide his light under a bushel. He set forth his own convictions on diet and also the teachings Mother White had advocated in conformity with what God had revealed to her. He told his students that he enjoyed excellent health on a vegetarian diet. A number of his students began to follow his example. To avoid embarrassment, management at the college provided two vegetarian tables in the dining room, but this arrangement did not settle the matter.

President Prescott called Edward Sutherland into the office where the young professor confronted not only the president, but also the matron of the institution.

"Edward, we appreciate your work as Bible teacher, but you must realize that you should avoid discussion of matters that may lead to controversy and fanaticism." The president looked at him with compassionate eyes. "You do understand, don't you?"

Then the matron spoke up. "Edward, I'm surprised that you would stir up the students over a matter so trivial."

Edward did not argue, neither did he yield. His convictions stood, and his students stood with him. Within three years the president had become a vegetarian himself and meat disappeared from the Battle Creek College dining room never to reappear.

Both Edward Sutherland and Percy Magan counted it a great blessing to be associated with President Prescott. They recognized his profound intellect and his great piety. He sometimes thought so deeply that his young colleagues could not follow, but this circumstance increased their respect for him. He had undertaken the presidency of Battle Creek College when it was young, unformed, and unstable. He had brought it to stable and organized maturity. But President Prescott never quite threw off the shackles of his classical education.

"I understand that when this college was established, Mother White counseled against locating it in the city," Edward said to Percy as they walked together toward their classrooms one day. The matter had been on his mind for some time.

"Yes, as far back as that she urged them to locate in the country," Percy agreed.

"I heard that when she got back to Battle Creek after a long absence in California, she heard that the college would be located in the city of Battle Creek and she sat down and cried."

Percy thought for a while. "I'm sure Mother White has wept many tears because God's people are so slow to act on the directions He sends us through her."

They reached their building, and Edward spoke the final word. "Well, I thank God she stood by the college anyhow, and ever since that time she has continued to send warnings and pleadings for them to do what God wants them to do."

A wave of nostalgia hit Edward. Mother White had left for Australia; and although her letters came frequently, bringing warnings and encouragement, it wasn't the same as having her near where they could run in and ask questions and have prayer with her. Edward kept wondering just what would have happened if the educational leaders had followed her counsel and done what God asked. A longing grew in his heart to be connected with an educational institution that would follow God's guidance all the way.

It seemed impossible that the college could now be pried away from Battle Creek. Crippled by its location, it could not possibly follow the counsel Mother White had given about making agriculture "the A, B, and C of education." Grieved and disappointed she had turned from her beloved Battle Creek and gone to Australia on the other side of the world. There she saw an opportunity to found a school according to the outline God had revealed to her. Avondale School, at Cooranbong, Australia, came forth under her care and guidance to bless the whole world.

Edward knew that the church and the leaders in Battle Creek felt some remorse over the past, a present aching loneliness, a spiritual emptiness, and growing concern for the future.

Edward recalled President Prescott's words right after the Harbor Springs Convention. "We have now given the Lord a chance to work more according to His mind, and less according to our ideas."

Edward knew that the battle line in every spiritual reform or revival is drawn between the mind of God and the ideas of men. Yet the years when counsel should have been heeded had passed into eternity. The right plans that should have prevailed had been locked within the messages from God's servant but not carried into operation. Edward and his friend Percy often talked about the problem and joined their prayers in earnest supplication that God's will might be done in the college and in all other areas of the growing work. Both men showed unusual promise; both had vision, wisdom, and faith. Both had taken their stand firmly on the message of righteousness by faith. It had taken hold at the very roots of their experience, and the passing years only served to deepen and strengthen their certainty that God could and would "work out in them that which was well-pleasing in His sight."

When spring came again, Edward went home to Sally one day with news that they were being transferred again—this time to the far West.

"Whatever line of investigation we pursue, with a sincere purpose to arrive at truth, we are brought in touch with the unseen, mighty Intelligence that is working in and through all."—*Education,* p. 14.

A COLLEGE IN THE NORTHWEST

When Edward Sutherland had entered Battle Creek College as a student in 1886, the church had three schools: Battle Creek College in Michigan, Healdsburg College in California, and South Lancaster Academy in Massachusetts. The following year a few scattered but determined Seventh-day Adventists launched two new academies on the raw frontier of the great Northwest; the North Pacific Academy in east Portland and the Milton Academy in the northeastern part of Oregon, a few miles south of the Washington Territory border.

Attendance at both of these new academies surprised everyone and generated an urge for a college. The head of the educational department came to Portland in the spring of 1890, and on a Sabbath morning, May 13, he presented a special message from Ellen G. White on the subject of a school for the Pacific Northwest. The school must be a college. As a result of this message the two academies surrendered their rights so that the new college might be born.

Much deliberation and prayerful planning followed. The leaders selected a committee of thirteen to consider and give final approval to the project. Then a locating committee of seven chose a site just outside Walla Walla, Washington. Finally a finance committee of nine presented a report to the General Conference assembled in Battle Creek, Michigan, in March of 1891. On March 11 the General Conference approved it and Walla Walla College had its beginning.

Much preparation needed to be made, buildings had to be erected, a staff of workers had to be assembled, essential equipment had to be readied before the new college could open its doors. The General Conference chose young Edward Sutherland to direct the newborn institution as principal, designating Prescott as president of both Battle Creek College and the new institution. In July of 1892 the Sutherlands arrived on campus.

As principal of the college, Ed faced a herculean task. A curriculum had to be prepared, and a catalog had to be printed. A full teaching staff had to be secured, and prospective students must be contacted. Besides all this he had the job of exercising oversight of the laborers who worked diligently to complete the college building.

In the midst of unpacking and getting settled in their new home, Edward and Sally talked over school plans. "It is hoped we can open the college in January, but we can't wait that long," Edward remarked, shaking his head.

"Why not?" Sally looked around at the clutter of packing cases.

"Because we must complete two terms this first year and we can't do it unless we begin early in December."

"Well, in spite of that—" Sally picked up another armload of linen and then went on— "I suppose we must go to the one camp meeting still scheduled for the summer. It's in Seattle, isn't it?"

"Yes, it is, and I agree. We must do all we can to promote the college and to contact students and get acquainted with our church people here in the Northwest. We have undertaken a gigantic task."

Principal Sutherland not only attended the Seattle camp meeting, but he also spent some time traveling among the churches and doing all he could to ensure a good attendance at the beginning of the school session. He had set December 7 as the target date. To make sure that this date would be met, the workmen put in long hours. Carpenters, plumbers, electricians, and plasterers worked in an atmosphere of speed and enthusiasm. When Wednesday, the seventh of December, dawned, one question loomed in the minds of all, "Will we have school today?"

The morning passed slowly. Light snow had fallen the night before graciously covering the bare ground, softening the starkness of the unfinished buildings.

At eleven o'clock the big bell in the belfry rang out. Ninety-one students with ten teachers, several board members, and many visitors from the young settlement of College Place filed into the chapel. There, with hearts overflowing with enthusiasm and thankfulness for this new educational center,

51

they praised God for His great goodness. Then the students gave themselves over to examinations and classification necessary for placement in classes.

On Monday morning, December 12, they convened for their first formal session. The students climbed the rough stairway and took their chapel seats as they would continue to do the rest of the school year in their regular school program. A heating stove had been installed in the chapel. Its chimney stuck out the center window in the back of the room. This stove and the borrowed range in the kitchen furnished the only heat in the building. Gradually, however, order evolved from chaos, and soon all had settled into their program of work with the contentment and smooth efficiency that has since characterized Walla Walla College in all its operations.

The first meal in the college dining room consisted of white crackers and milk. When the cook tried to use the borrowed range, nothing but smoke emerged. The hundred or so students and teachers were served in an unheated dining room.

A stark four-story building was used for offices, classrooms, and housing for some of the faculty. At the back of the building on either side were wings—one for the men's dormitory, the other for the women's. Between the two wings was the tin-roofed kitchen and dining area.

Edward Sutherland thanked God for all that had been accomplished, but the thought of what still needed to be done almost overwhelmed him. How could the faculty conduct effective classes in an unheated building with the noise of hammers pounding all day long, along with the rasp of the saw and all the jumble of sounds usual on a large unfinished building. Yet somehow everyone carried on.

One evening when Edward went to the apartment, he noticed the bed blocking a doorway. "Why have you pulled our bed in front of the door?" he asked Sally, a quizzical look on his face.

Sally laughed, "You know there isn't a lock in this building and we have taken in quite a lot of money in tuition." She lifted the pillow on the bed as she spoke. "My safe-deposit box is in this bed." She showed him where she had hidden the college funds. "You know how hard it is to get to the bank. It rains all the time, and the roads are terrible."

Her husband smiled. His Sally could manage anything. She already held the position of matron and had begun to mother all the dormitory students. Now she had become treasurer too. "How do the students like the vegetarian food?" Edward asked, changing the subject. "Have you heard any complaints?"

Sally's face lighted with her sparkling smile. "They seem to enjoy the food. Miss Giddings is an excellent cook." She licked her lips. "Do you realize that the fruit and vegetables in this valley are something special? Did you ever taste such butter beans or such delicious honey or apples?"

Edward nodded his agreement. "I notice that Mr. Hobbs is turning out some especially tasty bread and rolls and other delicious things in that bakery of ours."

"Yes, the wheat in this valley seems to have excellent qualities. Our students are so fortunate." Sally looked into Edward's face with that childlike expression of wonder that he loved so much.

"I'm sure that God is blessing us because we have determined to serve the students a strictly vegetarian diet."

Edward thought for a moment, then he spoke in a lower tone. "Sally, do you know that this is the first Seventh-day Adventist institution to serve the diet God intended for mankind?" He realized more than ever that God had led the committee in choosing this land—this acreage literally flowing with milk and honey.

One thing troubled Edward Sutherland more than he cared to admit. He knew that the original school farm the committee purchased had consisted of 120 acres. So pinched had the finances of the project become, that the men in charge had sold off parcel after parcel of the land until only a small portion of the original acreage remained. This had been done before the Sutherlands had arrived in the West to take over direction of the college. In his mind he saw the old mistakes of Battle Creek being reenacted here at Walla Walla, and his heart cried out to God for remedy. He prayed with Sally every day about this most urgent of problems.

One thing he could do, he could instruct his faculty in the teachings God had sent through Mother White regarding Christian education. So he held retreats where the faculty members studied the testimonies relating to the subject, and the Bible principles began to emerge clearly before their eyes and minds.

The men and women of the small faculty directing this new college found these principles looming before them with such drawing power that they discussed them constantly and studied how they might bring this institution into conformity with God's plan.

Principal Sutherland knew that without sufficient land the college could never meet the standard set in Mother White's instruction. Now political events, though disastrous to the nation, worked to bring about Edward Sutherland's dream of an adequate farm for Walla Walla College. President Benjamin Harrison's comfortable administration drew to a close, but already sinister shadows of coming financial collapse fell across the nation. The farmers who had purchased the college land could not meet their payments, and Principal Sutherland bought back eighty acres. Now Mr. Huddleston, the farm manager, could begin to develop the gardens, orchards, and fields that should go with a college like Walla Walla.

The girls' dormitory contained one bathroom and one tub. The boys' dormitory had similar accommodation. The faculty authorized a letter to the General Conference telling of the bathroom situation and asking for help. They received an answer giving them specific and detailed instructions on how to take a bath in a wash basin. Each dormitory room was then equipped with a basin and a pitcher.

Sutherland built a Dutch oven for the kitchen. He did everything he could to provide necessary conveniences for the students and to foster a spirit of cheerful acceptance of the hard things they must face. He got up at five o'clock each morning to handle his end of the crosscut saw, with a student as his partner. A great deal of wood had to be cut to supply the needs of the institution, and Sutherland did his full share of the hard work.

Thus he demonstrated one of his firm principles—that all teachers and all students should spend some time every day working together at productive manual labor.

He remembered an important thing that Mother White had said. "If the youth can have but a one-sided education, a knowledge of the sciences or a knowledge of labor for practical life, let it be the latter."

So fully had Edward Sutherland embraced her philosphy of education that he not only studied and taught it, but he practiced it every day in every way possible.

The first school year, which started in such confusion and under so many difficulties, prospered beyond the fondest hopes of the most ardent enthusiasts. Within two months the enrollment had increased to 165. The rooms were occupied as fast as the carpenters finished them. A Walla Walla annual records:

"On June 20, 1892, the Seventh-day Adventist constituency of the Pacific Northwest was listed as 1551. That year Whitman College in Washington had been in operation twenty-five years, ten as a college. It had around one hundred students. The previous year's report for the University of Washington, in its thirtieth year, was ten teachers and forty-two college students. In the light of these facts, the progress made that year in the unfinished building of Walla Walla College is the more remarkable."

The young educator weighed these matters in his mind and discussed them often with Sally. They saw in them the manifest blessing of God.

During the closing exercises of the first school

year, held on the campground at Milton, Oregon, Edward Sutherland and one of his teachers, Cassius Hughes, were ordained to the gospel ministry.

Despite worsening economic conditions, Walla Walla College entered its second year with bright hopes. Although the average student attendance dropped to only 105, thus posing a financial problem, the administration increased its teaching staff to twelve, half of them new.

George Droll, husband of Edward Sutherland's sister Lydia, came to be the college preceptor and to teach science. Lydia taught Greek and Latin classes. They brought with them a young lady, M. Bessie DeGraw, who had just finished a year at Battle Creek College. She should have continued her studies at Battle Creek, but Professor Prescott had asked her to assist as a teacher at the new college in Walla Walla. She agreed to go, provided she would not be asked to serve as preceptress. She joined the Drolls, and the three of them traveled west by train. At Walla Walla the Sutherlands met Miss DeGraw for the first time. No one could look into the piquant face with its roguish smile and fail to discern the strength of mind and character that resided in this remarkable young woman. And Edward Sutherland asked her to be preceptress of Walla Walla College. This, she had resolved never to do; however, Edward Sutherland's powers of persuasion prevailed over the strongminded M. Bessie DeGraw, and for the next four years she carried the work of preceptress along with her history classes. Edward Sutherland also influenced her to accept his ideas of Christian education and his philosophy of life in such a measure that for the next sixty years she would support all his projects and policies with every power at her command.

The second year the college offered courses in cooking, printing, gardening, and dairying. Two four-year courses were offered: scientific and classical. Students could help earn their tuition by cutting timber in the mountains above Milton, Oregon. The timber the college bought and hauled to Walla Walla.

During the fall term of the second year, President Prescott spent a week at the college and declared that he found everything in good shape. At that time he gave up his title as president of the college to Edward A. Sutherland, who had been directing the school from its beginning. Now Sutherland became president in name as well as in office.

During the college's third year, short courses were offered for those young people who wished to make speedy preparation to enter the Lord's work. President Sutherland had read that "young men who design to enter the ministry should not spend a number of years solely in obtaining an education."

The enrollment greatly increased, due to the many students taking advantage of the shorter courses. President Sutherland attributed both financial and spiritual progress to a faculty devoted to the light given to Ellen G. White. They diligently studied the articles on education coming from Australia, especially during 1895 and 1896. The faculty, though overloaded with school duties, took time to study together the principles of educational reform. The messages inspired them; so did

M. Bessie DeGraw, who stood by Dr. E. A. Sutherland and his ideals of Christian education throughout the years.

reports of the new Avondale School, built on land which the Lord had chosen and now operating on the new educational principles. In humble faith President Sutherland undertook to model Walla Walla College after the Avondale School in Australia.

In their studies the faculty discovered that finding and knowing truth without prompt and willing obedience could be a snare instead of a blessing. They pledged themselves to follow the light wherever it might lead. This decision required strong faith and courage, but it led them to the mountaintop where, with extended vision, they could evaluate the advantages of the new education and compare it with past experience when the counsel of God had been neglected. Under the inspiration of the God-guided plan they followed on through trust to triumph in educational leadership and reform.

President Sutherland did stand staunchly for reform, but nothing in the record of those days indicates that he expected or desired promotion because of it. In February of 1897, however, the General Conference session listened with rapt attention to a report from the young president of Walla Walla College. He told them of the prayerful study that he and his faculty had made of the inspired instruction on education, of the light that burned in their hearts, and how they were shaping their college program to conform to the new light on Christian education. So inspired was his presentation, so convincing the words he chose, and so appealing the message he bore that his fellow educators and the church leaders were impressed. Before the General Conference session ended, they had elected Edward A. Sutherland to be president of his alma mater, Battle Creek College in Michigan.

> **"True education is a grand science, for it is founded on the fear of the Lord, which is the beginning of wisdom."**—*Fundamentals of Education*, p. 528.

CHANGING TIMES

In the early part of the nineteenth century a religious awakening began in America. By the middle of the century the sixty institutions of higher learning representing the major Protestant denominations in the United States felt the need for reform.

John Jay Shipherd and a friend had collaborated and formulated a scheme for schools to have manual labor as a part of their program. He suggested these schools be set up away from cities. With this idea in mind Oberlin College in Ohio was founded. Oberlin became established as a center of reform. The Bible replaced pagan philosophy and literature. Other schools were located in rural settings, and education was more individualized. Farming became a vital activity. Manual labor became more and more important in character development and for student support. New attention became focused on health reform as well.

However, by the middle of the century, the educational reformers had become "weary in well doing." A historian looking back branded the reform advances as "foibles."

Ellen G. White in 1872 had published a courageous thrust against the orthodox trends of her time. With holy boldness, born of her consciousness of her role as a messenger of truth, she had pressed her views on her church. Its leaders, only partly convinced, followed her lead with feeble and faltering footsteps. For twenty years she had urged, counseled, warned; then she left for Australia where she demonstrated in the Avondale School what the educators in America had not been able to grasp.

Although Ellen White had gone to Australia, she did not cease to advise, warn, and instruct by published articles and many letters. In 1891 she wrote: "Should Christ enter our institutions for training of our youth, He would cleanse them as He cleansed the temple."

In June 1896 she spoke again to the Battle Creek College, church center for the denomination: "Oh, if ever a temple on earth needed purifying, the institutions in Battle Creek need it now."

The following November Elder O. A. Olsen made the following admission in the Battle Creek church: "From time to time, this church and these institutions have received very solemn and important messages of warning and instruction, but these messages have not received the careful attention they deserve, and the reformation they call for has not been made."

Just before the General Conference session opened in College View, Nebraska, Ellen G. White wrote from Australia on January 8, 1897: "To my brethren in America. . . . Oh, if I could have the joyful news that the will and minds of those in Battle Creek who have stood professedly as leaders, were emancipated from the teachings and slavery of Satan, whose captives they have been for so long, I would be willing to cross the broad Pacific to see your faces once more. But I am not anxious to see you with enfeebled perceptions and clouded minds because you have chosen darkness rather than light."

Although the leaders at Battle Creek had not acted on the counsel Ellen G. White had given, nevertheless God did send His Holy Spirit to move on the hearts of the students at the college, and she wrote in 1896: "The Lord God of heaven has caused His Holy Spirit from time to time to move on the students in the school, that they might acknowledge Him in all their ways, so that He might direct their paths. At times the manifestation of the Spirit has been so decided that studies were forgotten and the greatest Teacher the world ever knew made His voice heard."

During the four years, from 1893-1896, Edward Sutherland, the young president of Walla Walla College, carried his faculty with him into diligent study of those messages coming out of Australia, while with earnest prayer and sincere dedication they put those teachings into practice in their college.

Then, through the providence of God in 1897, the Sutherlands and their trusted co-worker, M. Bessie DeGraw, were transferred to Battle Creek

College, where Edward joined his old friend Percy T. Magan. Miss DeGraw united with Sutherland and Magan, forming a trio that worked together through Edward Sutherland's lifetime to carry on those educational reforms advocated by Ellen G. White.

On July 27 in the Tabernacle church at Battle Creek Percy Magan was ordained to the gospel ministry. His friend, Edward Sutherland, preached the sermon. Now the way had been fully prepared for these two educators to go forward united in dedicated obedience to the light on education that had come through Ellen G. White.

Percy Magan, who had been on the Battle Creek faculty for several years, offered strong support to the new president, Edward Sutherland. Under their leadership the college altered its course of study. The curriculum became more flexible, enabling the students to choose the subjects they desired. The Review and Herald of November 1, 1897, carried an announcement from President Sutherland offering short courses for mature students, missionary workers, teachers, bookkeepers, and canvassers.

A general reorganization of the college included setting up a new corporation in order to prohibit the college from conferring academic degrees. The situation soon became critical. Faculty members who had served under the former management found difficulty in adjusting to the radical reforms being introduced by the young president. The students also had a hard time rethinking ideas which had become well settled in their minds. And President Sutherland, now a young man of thirty-two, caught between the pressure of inertia on one hand and his own burning convictions on the other, had the most severe trial of all.

Into this tense situation came these startling words from Australia: "Now as never before we need to understand the true science of education. If we fail to understand this, we shall never have a place in the kingdom of God. 'This is life eternal, that they may know thee, the only true God, and Jesus Christ whom thou hast sent.' If this is the price of heaven, shall not our education be conducted on these lines?"

This statement from Mother White heartened the young president and placed the issue in clear perspective. Like Paul, he conferred not with flesh and blood, but hastened to obey the heavenly vision.

Percy Magan stood beside him. Together they shared the vision, and together they were obedient. They encouraged one another in the Lord. "Percy, God will not let any man or any group of men defeat us if we stand stiffly for what is right," Edward told his friend while they walked together across the campus. "We may have to pass through hard places, but God will prosper us if we take our stand on the *Testimonies.*"

Percy Magan thought for a moment. "Why is it so hard for so many of these good people to see that the *Testimonies* are a revelation from God?"

The two friends walked on with their resolution strengthened that they would follow the light revealed by Mother White, come what would.

President Sutherland's powers of persuasion proved to be great enough and inspired enough to enable him to carry out his reforms and go forward

65

with his program. Sometimes he advanced faster than his co-workers could follow; but on the whole, remarkable changes took place, and genuine improvement ensued.

"How can God's plan for a college be carried out on a seven-acre campus?" President Sutherland asked his advisers. "And in the city too." When President Sutherland looked over the tiny campus and thought of the wide acres at Walla Walla, he also thought of Mother White's counsel, "Study in agricultural lines should be the A, B, and C of the education given in our schools." He realized how far short of God's ideal this college had fallen.

Nearly twenty years earlier Ellen White had counseled the leaders in Battle Creek on the importance of having land for cultivation as part of the college training, also workshops in the charge of men who were competent to instruct the students in the varied aspects of physical labor. She warned them that much would be lost if they failed to unite physical effort with mental labor, and she warned against allowing the students to occupy their leisure hours with frivolous pleasures "which weaken the moral powers."

Sutherland and Magan surveyed the crowded conditions on the campus and resolved to do something even on this restricted campus of seven acres—including a tennis court. "Let's turn the tennis court and the baseball diamond into a vegetable garden," Edward Sutherland suggested.

"I'll help you." Percy Magan rolled up his sleeves.

So President Sutherland held the plow, Magan drove the team, and 225-pound J. G. Lamson sat on the beam while they plowed up the recreation area and made it into a vegetable garden.

Then their faith and zeal met with a reward. Friends of the institution donated the money to purchase an eighty-acre farm. Of course the new acreage lay at some distance from the campus, but with inspired enthusiasm the apostles of reform set to work. They set out fruit trees, shrubs, and vines on thirty acres, and the remainder they planted to vegetable, legume, and root crops that would supply the college with fresh produce. The new farm also furnished work for students. A number of them earned part of their tuition, and many more would be given work in the future. The college intended to bring the farm to its highest potential of production. Then a statement appeared in the *Advocate* like a flag floating over the reform movement: "The work of cultivating the soil, planting trees, vines and seeds is educational in the highest sense."

Every aggressive reform meets obstacles and comes to a slowdown. The Battle Creek College reform movement was no exception. Such crises try the mettle of the reformers and reveal their true measure. In such hours a man must turn to a Source higher than himself for solace and fortitude. His courage must carry him through with faith undimmed, with tolerance toward his opposers, and with compassion toward the deserters and the blind who cannot see. It must have been at this time that the thirty-five-year-old president found a bit of poetry that became his inspiration through all his after years:

"Then be content, poor heart;
    God's plans like lilies pure and white unfold.

We must not tear the close-shut leaves apart—
   Time will reveal the chalices of gold."

"Chalices of gold," the full-blown glory of the reform, accomplished and perfected—how Sutherland and his supporters longed for it!

To these leaders, Sutherland and Magan, every challenge demanded a decision to believe and to act on that behalf. It also demonstrated a constant need to wrestle with God in prayer. Often President Sutherland and his wife, with Percy Magan and Miss DeGraw, would retire to their prayer room on the second floor. There they agonized with their Lord that the right thing might be done in the right way. Shoulder to shoulder with these four stood Alonzo T. Jones, chairman of the board, and Dr. J. H. Kellogg, medical director of Battle Creek Sanitarium just across the street from the college.

Others also lent their support to the reform movement: Homer R. Salisbury, who later became an educational leader; C. M. Christiansen, who headed industrial training at the school; Frederick Griggs, educational leader who saw clearly the need for church schools; J. E. Tenny, E. D. Kirby, Stephen Haskell, and others. Supporting this local nucleus at Battle Creek were many other church leaders in the field.

> "True education. . . . is the harmonious development of the physical, the mental, and the spiritual powers. It prepares the student for the joy of service in this world, and for the higher joy of wider service in the world to come."—*Education,* p. 13.

PRISONERS OF HOPE

The August *Advocate* of 1899, published at Battle Creek College, discussed the Catholic view of education and quoted from a Roman Catholic pamphlet: "The conferring of degrees was originated by a pope."

This challenge stirred the faculty into action. They forthwith announced: "The College, under its new organization, ceases, with this year to grant degrees. Preparation for usefulness in the cause of Christ will be the subject constantly held before students, replacing the courses and diplomas of the past."

On the same page with this announcement two interesting statements appeared. President Sutherland read over the one: "After two years of emphasis on practical education, on industrial training, this last graduating class to receive degrees has nineteen members—one each in scientific, classical, Bible, and English departments, eight in sacred music, and seven piano graduates."

He let the paper fall to his lap. "Rather a poor showing for all our reform efforts," he said to his wife, Sally.

Sally looked up at him with a bright smile. "It's a bit early to expect drastic results. God is working. Wait and see."

He picked up his paper and read on: "The first finishing class of the American Medical College held its Battle Creek closing exercises on the College campus, Sunday afternoon, June 18. The degree of M.D. will be granted in Chicago, as the institution is incorporated under the laws of the state of Illinois."

Paradox? Yes. But reforms come slowly and sometimes go to extremes.

The dedicated educational leaders at Battle Creek faced their enormous problems with courage and conviction that grew into a passion. They spoke, they wrote, they prayed. They had spent five years in studying; the time had come for action. Now the scope of reform widened and deepened. The *Advocate* had been born the previous January, an ambitious little crusader of fifty-two pages, five by seven inches in size. Under its title it announced its purpose: "Devoted to the interests of Battle Creek College, a training school for Christian workers." It soon became the organ of the educational work of the church and within three years it had also become the organ of the Sabbath School Department. Beginning with its second year it was renamed *The Training School Advocate* and appeared in a larger page size. Edward Sutherland edited the paper, and M. Bessie DeGraw assisted. Percy Magan published it.

Encouraged, they discovered that the written word is a powerful weapon of reform. In October of 1900 the *Advocate* announced a new book by Professor Sutherland, a 400-page volume published by the Review and Herald and entitled *Living Fountains or Broken Cisterns.* This thoughtful and well-researched work traced the conflict between true and false education from the Eden school, through the experiences of ancient Israel, down through the perversions of the pagan world and the papal influence for a thousand years. Then the impact of the Protestant Reformation was set forth, together with the Catholic reaction, bringing the issue down to the end of the nineteenth century, where it faced Christian educators of that time. Among them stood Edward Alexander Sutherland with his eyes open and his face set like a flint to stem the decadent tide.

Self-effacing Miss DeGraw usually worked behind the scenes, content if only the reform to which she had dedicated all her resources and talents moved forward at a healthy pace. She assisted President Sutherland in the research and writing of the book, *Living Fountains or Broken Cisterns.* When Alonzo Jones read the manuscript before publication, he remarked to President Sutherland, "There is a woman in that book."

"The woman" and her editorial ability were recognized and appreciated. Later, Miss DeGraw helped S. N. Haskell on his two volumes, *The Story of Daniel the Prophet* and *The Story of the Seer of Patmos.*

71

Perhaps not so prominent as the young president of Battle Creek College, but certainly as active and important in the promotion of educational reform, was Percy Magan, dean of the college. The two worked together, and Magan's part proved vital and valuable. He wrote many articles for the *Advocate* and other church publications. He had published a book a year earlier than Sutherland, *The Peril of the Republic,* brought out by Fleming H. Revell. All the proceeds from the sale of this book Percy Magan donated to assist in paying off the college debt.

Under Sutherland and Magan's leadership, Battle Creek College altered its course of study. They offered shorter courses so that students could prepare themselves quickly for missionary service. President Sutherland had announced in November 1897, that the college administration would provide winter school of twelve weeks, complete in itself. "Everything will be done to carry on this course so that it will be adapted to the needs of those who have good reasons for not spending more time in school."

In January 1899 great emphasis began to be centered on a regular, consistent student missionary routine. The college established a mission in the city of Jackson, about 40 miles east, where eight students served from two to four weeks, treating the sick, ministering to the needy, and holding meetings in the evening. Homer Salisbury, one of the faculty members, directed this project. Other students carried on similar work in the city of Battle Creek.

All the changes that came in, some abrupt, some gradual, were brought to pass by the spirit that impelled the movement. The movement of reform had a soul. It did not come from mere enthusiasm, but from thorough conviction based on vision. Many good people in Battle Creek, in the school and out, did not share the opinions or approve of the reforms undertaken by the new administration. Some of them drew back.

President Sutherland, Dean Percy Magan, and the reformers who rallied to their cause pressed the issues with patient persistence. To them it loomed as a life-and-death matter.

The reform movement ran into formidable opposition. Since reform in education meant discarding certain servilities toward the classical trend, many students objected. Those who were short on vision and long on worldly ambition rebelled and threatened to leave in a body to join another college. Disapproval arose from many directions, and criticism rained down on the devoted but unprotected heads of the leaders. What should they do? Should they retreat from their position? No, never! They heard in their minds like the thunder from ancient Sinai the warning of 1897: "Now as never before we need to understand the true science of education. If we fail to understand this, we shall never have a place in the kingdom of God."

They chose to maintain their position, to make straight paths for their feet with no faltering or turning aside. God honored their steadfast action. The heroic dedication of loyal students and teachers brought down heavenly blessing. Reform resulted in progress that everyone could see. Financial relief came too; but most thrilling of all, spiritual revival came.

When Edward Sutherland came to take over direction of the college in the spring of 1897, a huge debt of almost $100,000 lay on it like a crushing weight. While this deficit had been accumulating through previous administrations over a period of several years, the burden fell on Sutherland and Magan. They accepted it and began to cope with it.

In 1899 the General Conference held its session in South Lancaster, Massachusetts. It had concluded its business; and the delegations, including most of the General Conference men, boarded a train bound for Battle Creek. A porter came through the cars waving a telegram. It proved to be from the college. President Sutherland read it aloud: "STUDENTS RAISE ALMOST SIX THOUSAND DOLLARS TO APPLY ON COLLEGE DEBT."

Such a wave of excitement and joy went through the company of delegates that every person aboard the train was affected. Ed Sutherland and Percy Magan looked into each other's eyes and read there a reflection of his own delight. Nothing but the Spirit of God could have accomplished such a thing.

Later the *Advocate* reported: "When the delegates reached Battle Creek to carry on the legal proceedings, about thirty-five were entertained in the College Home. Here they came in contact with the students, and they expressed themselves as pleased with the spirit pervading the school.

"The day before their arrival, the students had taken hold of the college debt and in cash and pledges nearly six thousand dollars had been raised."

When all the gifts and pledges had been

74

counted, including a generous remission of interest due the Review and Herald, the amount totaled $22,211, to which were added later the proceeds from certain amounts of labor and certain acres of land dedicated to this cause.

Just a year later, in the spring of 1900, a new and substantial source of relief developed. Ellen White dedicated her book *Christ's Object Lessons* to the relief of Battle Creek College and other debt-ridden schools. All the royalty income went for this purpose, also all income received from its sale by the Review and Herald. The Review even furnished the materials and donated the labor.

Percy Magan formed a committee, Relief of the Schools, and became its secretary and chief promoter. Hundreds of workers and laymen, even children, entered the campaign and sold books by the thousands. At the 1901 General Conference, Percy Magan reported that about $57,000 had already been raised by the sale of *Christ's Object Lessons* in America, also plates had been shipped to Australia and England, and plates were being prepared for Scandinavia and Germany. Under Magan's enthusiastic leadership the plan proved a godsend to the schools.

More important than financial relief was the spiritual revival that blessed the churches, and Battle Creek in particular. And all the time the urgency toward reform pressed upon all hearts. Edward Sutherland still heard through all his prayers and meditations, that haunting message of 1897: "Now as never before we need to understand the true science of education."

Volume six of the *Testimonies for the Church* came from the press in 1901 and contained an eighty-three-page section on education. Its challenge came with fresh vigor. Like a diamond in its setting, one passage stood out in clear and sparkling luster:

"Though in many respects our institutions of learning have swung into worldly conformity, though step by step they have advanced toward the world, they are prisoners of hope. . . . If they will listen to His voice and follow in His ways, God will correct and enlighten them, and bring them back to their upright position of distinction in the world."—page 145.

To Edward Sutherland and his associates this message came as a command, a precept, and a promise. All across the land the young church took up the slogan, "Prisoners of Hope."

None of the reform leaders missed that "if" in the statement. "If they will listen to His voice and follow in His way." The conditions were simple, the terms were clear: Listen! Follow! Only then can God "correct and enlighten them." Only then can God "bring them back to their upright position," which is one "of distinction from the world."

With renewed zeal the men of Battle Creek took hold. They could allow no delay and no compromise. Educational reform must be carried forward to full triumph. As with young Josiah, ancient king of Judah, even "the high places" must at last be abandoned. Shoulder to shoulder, with united purpose, Edward Sutherland and Percy Magan set their faces "like a flint" toward victory, and along with them, behind the scenes as usual, for she was never a militant person, marched M. Bessie DeGraw.

"That our sons may be as plants grown up in their youth; that our daughters may be as corner stones, polished after the similitude of a palace."—Psalm 144:12.

THE LITTLE PEOPLE

The first two years of President Sutherland's administration at Battle Creek saw the birth and rapid growth of the Seventh-day Adventist church-school movement. January 28, 1899, was set apart for a day of special prayer. President Sutherland had written an article to be read in all the churches. In the evening after the devotions of the day were over, Edward and Sally talked it over. "Didn't they have a church school here in Battle Creek a long time ago?" Sally asked, as she pulled up a chair by the fire.

"Yes, they conducted a church school for one year just before the Civil War," her husband said as he settled himself in his easy chair. "Louisa Morton taught it. Then in 1860 John Fletcher Byington revived the Battle Creek church school."

"John Fletcher was the son of Elder John Byington, our first General Conference president, wasn't he?"

Edward nodded. "He had a deep interest in church schools too. He opened a church school in his home in Buck's Ridge, New York, and his daughter Martha taught it. That was in 1854."

"That must have been the first church school. And that was opened forty-five years ago. It has taken a long time to get that work started."

On into the night they discussed the urgent importance of the church schools. They decided that in the burning enthusiasm the pioneers felt for the newly espoused doctrines and the urge to spread them everywhere, they had overlooked the importance of training their children in the faith they held so dear. Now almost fifty years had passed.

Now another message came from Australia, where the heart and hand of Mother White were yielded every day to the work of guiding the infant church: "This work [church-school work] is fully as essential as the work for the older pupils. In localities where there is a church, a school should be established if there are no more than six children to attend."

For years she had been calling attention to this matter which had "long been neglected." Now a note of urgency thrilled through the words and spurred Edward Sutherland to action. There must be church schools. He must take prompt action.

Summer vacation, crowded with readjustments, passed quickly, and the new school year began. A gratifying number of students enrolled in the new normal department. The future of church schools began to look more hopeful, but the future seemed too far away. The need could not wait. A few churches were already calling for church-school teachers. The first call had come in the previous spring from Bear Lake, Michigan, the home of Albert Alkire. Two churches in Indiana now pressed their requests.

President Sutherland spread out the letters on his desk. He knew what Ellen G. White had said on this matter. Yonder, in the chapel, a sea of eager, young faces suggested the resources. But could any of these students interrupt their education? Dare he ask it of them? Would they respond?

With his usual forthright vigor, the young president sprang into action. First he enlisted the support of both the teaching faculty and the committee. Then he took his burden to the students in chapel. He told the students of a place that needed a teacher so much that he felt moved to ask if any student in the room would volunteer to break off his or her education and answer the call. No one responded. Edward Sutherland went to his knees in fervent supplication. The following morning he made his second appeal. A young lady rose and offered to go. Then two more students followed her example.

These first three volunteers laid aside their education in order to go to faraway churches and teach little boys and girls they had never seen. Maude Atherton went to Farmersburg, Indiana; Mattie Pease also went to an Indiana school; and Maude Wolcott (later Mrs. Arthur Spaulding) answered the call of the Alkire family in Bear Lake, Michigan. Within weeks others volunteered. Minnie Hart went to Milwaukee, Bertis A. Wolcott to Erie, Pennsylvania; Mae Pines taught the orphans in the Haskell Home in Battle Creek. By Christmas seven such schools were in operation, and by March thirteen had opened. Then a burst of energy seized the movement. During the following year fifty-seven church schools were organized. In the fall of 1900 nearly 150 schools opened their doors to the children of the growing church.

The church-school work had been launched on a permanent career, and President Sutherland had been, and continued to be, its chief promoter. He is regarded as the father of the Seventh-day Adventist church-school system. In Battle Creek, as president of the college, he sounded the clarion call to establish church schools. In a fiery speech at the General Conference in 1899 he said, "We call our older brethren out of Babylon, but we let our children attend Egyptian schools and learn Egyptian ways."

The February 1899 issue of the *Advocate*, official organ of the new reform movement at Battle Creek, reported: "One year ago the subject of church schools was but little thought about: today it has attracted the attention of every state in the Union."

The 1899 General Conference, held in South Lancaster, Massachusetts, actively launched the church-school movement. With such force and inspiration did President Sutherland and his supporters set forth the church's duty that it became a topic of conversation and prayer in Adventist homes across the land. The next General Conference, held in Battle Creek in April of 1901, made three recommendations:

"1. That we urge upon our people the importance of establishing church schools.

"2. That we recommend that our conference

laborers do not consider their work for the churches complete until church schools are organized wherever consistent.

"3. That we recommend the appointment of church-school superintendents in Union and State Conferences."

From Australia Ellen G. White looked upon these dramatic happenings and the official approval of the burgeoning church-school movement and endorsed it with all the fervor of her nature.

Perhaps the most radical step toward reform centered in the textbooks. When the General Conference formed the Department of Education in 1902, the educational leaders of the church were Edward A. Sutherland, Frederick Griggs, and C. C. Lewis. President Sutherland headed the central training school and, with M. Bessie DeGraw, provided the first elementary textbooks.

Much had been written in the literature of the church against pagan and skeptical sentiments in some of the texts used in public schools and advocating that the Bible should occupy first place as a textbook. Alonzo Jones, chairman of the board of Battle Creek College, and a high-ranking faculty member, advocated that the Bible should be "the textbook in physical science as well as in every other line of study."

Such a dramatic departure from educational patterns of the day stirred up formidable opposition. Enemies spread the story that all subjects—astronomy, biology, bookkeeping, mathematics, even banking, sewing, and cooking—would be taught with the Bible as the exclusive text. This report by enemies of the reform does not give a true picture and can be refuted on four points:

81

First, a statement by Ellen G. White: "The study of the sciences is not to be neglected. Books must be used for this purpose, but *they should be in harmony with the Bible for that is the standard."* (Italics supplied.)

Second, in his sermon at the close of summer school in 1899, Alonzo Jones said: "First of all, bear in mind that the Bible as the textbook in every study does not mean that the Bible is the *only* textbook in education."

Third, during the 1900 summer school at Battle Creek, a book committee was appointed to provide textbooks; so we know that other texts beside the Bible were approved and provided.

Fourth, in the *Advocate* of November 1903 the second edition of *Bible Reader* number one, is announced, prepared by Edward Sutherland and M. Bessie DeGraw. On the same page the *Advocate* advertises the price list of a full line of textbooks for church schools.

With Miss DeGraw, the young professor prepared between 1900 and 1904 a set of readers called the *Bible Readers.* Another text, *Mental Arithmetic,* authored by Edward Sutherland appeared in 1901. It does not resemble any arithmetic ever published. In contains problems about the bones of the body, about the difference in cost between beans and beefsteak, about distances in the Holy Land, about Old Testament chronology, about building a schoolhouse, about making out a canvasser's report, and about transactions and other practical matters. Young Adventists were taught how to figure their tithe. The last of the readers by Sutherland and DeGraw were printed in 1905.

"In such a place as Berrien Springs the school can be made an object lesson, and I hope that no one will interpose to prevent the carrying forward of the work."—Letter of Ellen G. White to managers of the Review and Herald office, July 12, 1901.

OUT ON THE LAND

The recent pointed messages from Ellen White hung over Sutherland and Magan with ominous significance. Both men sought to understand "the true science of education," without which they could not hope to attain eternal life. They studied and prayed over the matter constantly. The words describing the educational institutions of the church as "prisoners of hope" encouraged them, but they wondered how long God's people could wait without wearing out God's patience. Years of neglect and delay had already marred the history of Battle Creek College.

One day Magan brought the matter up again. "Ed, we must move the college out of Battle Creek."

"You are right, Percy." Ed Sutherland's far-seeing inner perception comprehended both the pressing need for change and also the many obstacles. "We must, but we can't. For now, we must wait."

In Edward Sutherland's nature a rare patience combined with tough persistence. He could wait in calm expectancy with vision undimmed and with ardor undiminished.

At the Michigan campground in the summer of 1898 President Sutherland had met Dr. David Paulson, patron saint of the Life Boat Mission in Chicago, editor of the *Life Boat,* and medical director of Hinsdale Sanitarium. The two men worked together interviewing students, scores of young people who wanted to attend Battle Creek College. After a day of such interviews, Dr. Paulson sighed and said, "How sad it is to find so many bright, promising young people who have no way to pay for a college education."

"It is most distressing," President Sutherland agreed. "Circumstances they cannot control deny them an education."

The two men walked through a hay meadow out toward the setting sun until a haystack hid them from the encampment of tents. They knelt there on its far side and laid the burden of their hearts before their Lord and entreated Him for wisdom and for light. They rose and Dr. Paulson spoke. "I believe I have a vision. You school men should move the college to a large farm and establish industries where students can earn their school expense."

"That's the message we've been getting from Mother White for years," Sutherland sighed. "It's not easy to do."

Dr. Paulson's voice raised a tone higher and he declared his fervent conviction. "I'd establish a school where no worthy student need be turned away, not even if he had to earn all his expenses, so long as he was willing to work for what he needed."

"Later, back at Battle Creek, Sutherland repeated this conversation to Percy Magan.

"Let's do it, Ed," Magan said. "Let's move Battle Creek College to a big farm and give worthy young people a chance.

After that they began to take secret trips on their bicycles, riding many miles with earnest entreaties to God on their lips that they might be led to the property that would best serve God's purpose.

The biennial session of the General Conference convened in Battle Creek in 1901. Ellen White had returned from Australia the year before and lived in California. She attended the General Conference session.

Christian education in general, and at Battle Creek in particular, received concentrated attention during this convocation. At one of the morning sessions Mother White gave a talk on the fundamentals of Christian education. Among other things she said: "Now a reform has begun in the college, why don't you do what you should have done when you established the college years ago, take it out of Battle Creek and establish it on a large farm, where it can develop along right lines. Although it may mean a fewer number of students, the school should be moved out of Battle Creek."

At the close of her talk the delegates met and voted that the General Conference authorize the college board to follow Mrs. White's advice and move the institution.

Edward Sutherland rejoiced. He felt that God had taken the matter into His own hands and that a green light had flashed on, indicating a forward move. The board appointed him and Percy Magan to carry out the General Conference recommendation and Ellen White's instructions. A committee composed of representatives from the General Conference and the college was appointed and empowered to choose and purchase a suitable location.

Systematic searching began at once. Edward and his wife, Sally, scoured the country on their bicycles. They went up and down the St. Joseph River. Once Sally went by herself by freight train to South Haven on Lake Michigan.

At times Edward took Percy Magan and others of the board members—searching for a place for the college. One day in May 1901 the men stacked their bicycles under an old maple on a plot of ground known as the Garland Farm. They stood on a bluff overlooking the dark waters of the St. Joseph River and the flat lands spreading out to the left known as the Richardson Farm.

Sutherland knew this area well; he had been here before. He led the other men down to the neglected Richardson place, then to the well-kept Garland Farm with its beautiful orchards, also to a wooded area known as Steven's Grove. The three farms totaled 274 acres. "This seems to be what we're looking for, " one man said.

"I believe God has led us to this place," another added his word. The committee voted to purchase the whole acreage and felt that they had done well. Most of the church members approved and agreed that the committee had made a wise choice.

Percy Magan declared what all the reformers felt, that a great victory had been won. He penned an enthusiastic description to Mother White: "The fruit farm will yield an immense income and is in such beautiful condition now that it will be an inspiration to our students to keep it in the same condition. The Richardson Farm will furnish a fine opportunity to make good land out of poor and run-down land, and the piece of woods will always be a magnificent place to hold our summer sessions of the General Conference . . . or educational assemblies. . . . A more quiet, peaceful and beautiful spot I have never seen."

Mother White answered: "I am much pleased with the description of this place. . . . In such a place as Berrien Springs, the school can be made an object lesson, and I hope no one will interpose to prevent the carrying forward of this work."

The new location lay only ninety miles from Battle Creek, but it could no longer bear the name of that city. They chose a new name, Emmanuel Missionary College. Dean Magan declared that the name epitomized the experience the committee had in locating the school; also it foreshadowed the school's future, "God with us."

Great joy filled the hearts of Edward Sutherland and his supporters. They felt that at last the right decision had been made and again God was leading them. Then, like Caleb and Joshua of old, Sutherland and Magan set out to conquer and subdue the new land.

"This new school," Magan wrote to Mother White, "must be the Avondale of America."

Although spring had already come, these men determined to begin classes in the new location that coming autumn. This stupendous task entailed moving all equipment, providing housing for faculty and students, and also preparing suitable classrooms. Only an Edward Sutherland and a Percy Magan would have believed it possible.

A month after the 1901 General Conference session closed, Battle Creek College held its twenty-fifth graduating exercises. Arthur G. Daniells, the new General Conference president, gave the commencement address. In it he delineated the type of education which a training school should provide and enumerated the advantages of the newly purchased location for the college. A few weeks later the General Conference approved the entire plan.

The leaders of the college regarded these decisions and pronouncements as their marching orders. They would do now what should have been done twenty-five years ago. Percy Magan acted fast. As soon as school ended in May, he packed and shipped sixteen freight cars of furniture, books, and other school equipment to Berrien Springs. By July 1 all had been deposited in an abandoned courthouse and jail. These quarters would serve as temporary classrooms and dormitories.

Summer school, called a "teachers' institute," they held that summer in tents pitched in the grove now called Indian Fields at the edge of the village on the banks of the river.

Two hundred elementary and secondary school teachers spent the summer at the camp in Indian Fields. Many General Conference Committee members visited the summer school and confessed that they were excited and thrilled with the promise of a school that dared to cut loose from traditional facilities and obey God's will by faith.

Possession of the land could not be taken until autumn, and the farm buildings were inadequate for school purposes; so for that year the college made do in the courthouse, while students and faculty found living quarters in the village, most of them in the old Hotel Roanoke.

That year they erected the first buildings in the beautiful but mosquito-infested maple woods behind the farmhouse and the proposed campus. These buildings consisted of small cottages and cabins and an assembly hall, octagonal in shape and screened for summer use. Percy Magan's wife gave the money—her whole inheritance from her father—for this hall.

As might have been expected, the uprooting of the college from Battle Creek in such a swift and spectacular manner produced a reaction. Ellen White had indeed told the school leaders to dispose of the school buildings as soon as possible and to find a place where right principles could be carried out.

The General Conference action endorsing her advice, however, was so sudden, so revolutionary, and so unexpected that it stunned many of the delegates. Reaction set in at Battle Creek. Some thought that regardless of what Ellen White said, the college should remain in Battle Creek. Some found their business interests threatened by the change. Reticence against change and blind devotion to status quo held many captive.

There was no rejoicing among church members to mark the departure from Battle Creek, no speeches or dinners or kindly farewells. The community at Battle Creek, as well as many who had been connected with the institution, objected to the move.

Facing such opposition, financial shortage, and a divided faculty along with the austerities of the new campus, Sutherland and Magan walked by faith alone.

Dr. David Paulson made the statement when he viewed the situation: "If there was ever an institution born without a golden spoon in its mouth, it certainly is the Berrien Springs school."

The first year in the new location saw fewer students enrolled. Ellen White had warned them that such would be the case. Nevertheless some of the brethren and even some of the college teachers took this decreased enrollment as an indication of failure.

But, as with Gideon's army, only those who were utterly committed to reform came to the new college as students, and they, of course, were a minority.

Not only did the critics object to the new location; they also objected to the new emphasis on the Word of God as the central authority in all lines of study. The new focus on the Bible seemed impractical to many students; and they, with a number of ministers, withdrew their support. They felt that Sutherland and Magan were wrong.

Were the two school leaders wrong in making God's Word the core of all learning? Ellen White clarified the whole situation in 1902: "Cautions were given to Brother Magan and Brother Sutherland against carrying their teaching so far above the spiritual level to which the students had been accustomed. . . . They were not to go so far in advance that it would be impossible for their students to follow them."

Observe that these words do not place Sutherland and Magan on the side of fanaticism; but on the central pathway of truth, although they had advanced too rapidly for the church members and students on a lower spiritual level to keep pace. Then she added: "I thank the Lord that these brethren heeded the instruction given them.

Since the president and the dean were both young, older more experienced brethren found it easy to criticize them. Only a month after moving the college, a college board session proposed that Elder W. W. Prescott replace Sutherland, because the latter "is young and inexperienced." Yet he had already been a successful president of two colleges before this one. Inexperienced?

During this trying crisis, Edward Sutherland and Percy Magan like David and Jonathan stood together. Magan defended the administration. "Educational reform had not been a mere theory with us," he said. They had wrestled with hard problems. He did not feel that other leadership should come in and change essential things pertaining to the college.

And Mother White also intervened. She told the church that Sutherland and Magan had been working "in the fear of God to carry out the principles of true education." She explained that, although these men were young, God desired to place them "on vantage ground." She rebuked their critics and assured them that God did not want these young men replaced by older ones.

Sutherland and Magan, conscious always of critics watching their every move, tried in every way to avoid occasions of offense.

One of their friends, seeing the advantage of cheap and easy water travel between St. Joseph and Benton Harbor, presented the school with a small boat which soon proved its worth. One day, when a delegation of visiting brethren was expected to visit the campus, President Sutherland called one of his trusted students. "Better hide that boat behind the shed—way down there where no one will see it."

He could have defended the boat, of course, but hiding it seemed easier—a demonstration of how Sutherland dealt with his critics. It also reveals what petty fuel fed their criticism on occasion.

Meantime, on the new campus, teachers and students united their efforts to farm and to build. Every faculty member accepted his post of leadership, teaching one half day and working with the students the other half. For the first time in Seventh-day Adventist history an institution built with student labor grew rapidly. Fifty or sixty students worked together under A. S. Baird, an experienced builder who had been called from ministerial work in Nebraska. He taught the students by working with them.

The business manager, C. M. Christensen, wished to build with bricks manufactured on the campus; but President Sutherland wanted plain, wooden structures with no attempt at beauty of design or artistic architecture. He wanted the buildings small and simple and with no heat or electricity, because the students would have to use such buildings in the mission field and they should get used to such accommodations. Life in such quarters "would discourage growth of pride and institutional spirit." These the president wished by all means to eliminate from the new institution to bring it into harmony with his understanding of God's plan.

This reform development at Berrien Springs marked the turning point in the educational history of the Seventh-day Adventist Church. The vision, courage, and resourcefulness demanded for the undertaking at Emmanuel Missionary College set shining examples for all other church schools to emulate. Within a year Elk Point Industrial School sprang up on the bank of the Missouri River in South Dakota. The founders located it on a farm with rich loam eighty feet deep. They patterned it after the new school in Berrien Springs. Other schools followed, and the influence spread even to foreign lands.

Avondale had set the example, Berrien Springs followed; and, because it had to break away from the stranglehold of the city and church headquarters, Emmanuel Missionary College may have had a great struggle. It broke with the popular trend in education and made new paths for its feet. Emmanuel Missionary College shattered the bands that bound the denominational schools to popular education.

"**Men of power are those who have been opposed, baffled, and thwarted. By calling their energies into action, the obstacles they meet prove to them positive blessings.**"—*The Ministry of Healing,* p. 500.

MEN OF GREAT FAITH

Sutherland and Magan had seen the General Conference pressed down under the enormous debt of Battle Creek College. They knew that institutional expansion had been undertaken without sufficient financial support. They resolved to make the new college self-supporting.

That first winter they faced a money shortage so desperate that the business office, with extreme difficulty, paid the teachers. Students endured hardships and inconveniences in their living quarters—the unheated cottages.

The president and his dean shared every responsibility, every burden, every crisis. Magan felt that it was necessary to take a month's vacation with relatives near Los Angeles in order to recover his health, but he could not bear the thought of leaving President Sutherland and Berrien Springs for so long. He feared that his friend could not endure the strain much longer. His absence left the college with no one at all to plan the new buildings, no one to gather the money to pay for them or to supervise their erection.

President Sutherland made many fund-raising trips while Percy Magan stayed "by the stuff," supervising the rapid development of the college. At one time Sutherland made plans to solicit money in the Northwest. The school, however, had no money to buy the railway ticket. The two men decided to go to Chicago (only a short distance) and solicit funds for the journey. Arriving at the railway station waiting room, Magan left President Sutherland sitting on a hard bench. "Ed you stay here and pray, even if it takes me the rest of the day." Then he headed for the railroad superintendent's office. To his surprise he saw that the superintendent sat at his desk pale and trembling. "You are in sorrow, perhaps," Magan said with genuine compassion. "Can you tell me about it?"

The man spent the next hour telling of the death of his two daughters and his wife's grave illness. Magan tried to comfort him.

Suddenly the official said, "This is not what you came to hear. What can I do for you?"

Magan made no haste to tell of his own need, but continued to speak of God's love and His willingness "to bear our grief and carry our sorrows." Then, with gentle tact, he explained the college's need, the purpose of their work, and that their building program could not continue unless the president could obtain donations from friends in the Pacific Northwest. He admitted that President Sutherland needed a ticket.

The superintendent signed a paper. Magan hurried to another office and rushed back to the waiting room to interrupt the prayers of President Sutherland with tickets for five separate trips to places he needed to go. Sutherland caught the afternoon train.

So often he spoke of his Lord. He seemed to have a very personal acquaintance with Him. His faith in the Lord was simple and sincere. How he loved to sing "Faith of Our Fathers"! He developed this experience through years of walking with God on his knees.

One such experience found him on his way to visit a friend in Oregon from whom he hoped to receive a large donation. He went up into a mountain to pray. On reaching the top of a high peak, a sense of loneliness and desolation came over him—an awe-inspiring impression of the nearness of eternity and the spirit world, resembling the thoughts which weigh upon the mind when watching alone with the dead.

The mingled murmur of a thousand torrents arose faintly from the dark cliffs and the deep gorges below. At intervals the prolonged and swelling roar of an avalanche interrupted the awful solitude, as with the rushing of invisible hosts trampling the barely discernable clouds and sweeping the pathless field of air.

The cold snow-shining peaks piercing the silent sky seemed like colossal monuments of a perished world standing alone in a wilderness of death. The utter absence of all sounds and forms of life—everything conspired to fill his soul with an oppressive sense of loneliness and desolation.

He continued to pray and humble himself before

his Maker. Suddenly, in the wee hours of the morning, the light began to break through, and the dark caverns disappeared to take the form of beautiful rock formations. The snow-covered peaks now shone like gigantic jewels, and the birds joined the babbling brooks in songs of praise, for the Dayspring had come. He felt relieved, and with a peaceful trust he fell asleep for a short time. He awoke fresh and revived as though he had slept all night. That day he was rewarded with the largest gift he had ever received.

The vision that Sutherland and Magan had held in their hearts and minds ever since 1895 had become to them the chief reason for their being. To learn and demonstrate the "true science of education" employed all their strength, their time, and their thought. The removal of the college to Berrien Springs had been a great step forward, and now they worked with every means at their command to nourish and build Emmanuel Missionary College.

The attempts made toward reform at Walla Walla and Battle Creek had taught these two educators that God's blessing does rest on those who obey His word, those who honor His prophets and submit their own will to His. The experience at Battle Creek had shown them that the way of reform is beset with opposition and criticism, even from those who profess belief in progress.

They had suffered severe criticism for their efforts to remove the college from Battle Creek, also for their heavy emphasis on the Bible as the source of all knowledge and the chief textbook for education in Christian schools.

When the college opened in the fall of 1903,

some three hundred persons lived on the campus. Three large homes of seven to nine rooms each had been finished, and teachers had already moved into them. They had built the Manual Arts building the year before and used its basement for kitchen and dining room. Its second story housed the college store and the carpenter shop. The newly erected Domestic Arts building provided housing for the college girls in its attic, while the boys were stowed in various attics and corners of other buildings.

The church schools still loomed large in President Sutherland's thinking, and he felt that they must provide more textbooks. Funds did not come in fast enough to push forward the work on the absolutely necessary buildings, let alone provide for the printing of new textbooks. The president and the dean had determined that they would build only as they had the funds in hand. There would be no repeat of the Battle Creek College debt. But they must have the textbooks, so President Sutherland, Miss DeGraw, and Percy Magan each borrowed $600. With this borrowed money they got out the textbooks.

The year 1903 had been eventful. Great changes had taken place throughout the whole denomination. In August the General Conference had moved from Battle Creek to establish its headquarters in Washington, D.C. The Review and Herald also moved at the same time. Percy Magan's wife, Ida, had sickened that spring and no medical help brought her much benefit.

Now severe criticism began to come from the newly established headquarters in Washington. Both Sutherland and Magan were bound to the church by ties of great strength and tenderness, and they walked in the glow of that great light behind them—the righteousness by faith message of 1888. They knew the touch of God's hand, and they knew His voice. Percy Magan expressed their attitude in his own words: "I know that these trials are sent to us, not to bring bitterness out of our characters, but to bring all the fragrance that God can possibly bring into our lives."

The holiday season of 1903 brought sorrow and loss to both the Sutherland and Magan families. Sutherland's "Aunt Nell" Druillard and her husband, Alvan, had lately returned from Africa where they had been engaged in mission work. Now they had settled in Berrien Springs, where they joined the college faculty and entered with enthusiasm into the reform program. Alvan Druillard sickened during December and passed away December 29.

Ida Magan spent all her time in the hospital now, while hopes for her recovery diminished with every passing day. The continual opposition heaped upon her husband and President Sutherland grieved and crushed her.

Sutherland and Magan learned that the Lake Union Conference intended to hold the spring session on the campus of Emmanuel Missionary College. They discussed their situation from all angles and decided that if no diminution of criticism should be evident before the conference should convene in May, they would resign their positions at that time.

Ida Magan passed to her rest on May 19 while the conference was in session. A few days later Ellen White spoke in the college church and praised Ida Magan's faithfulness. She blamed the cruel criticism and opposition that had been directed at Magan and Sutherland ever since they removed the college from Battle Creek to Berrien Springs. She said that this situation had weighted Ida Magan down with sorrow and "has cost the life of a wife and mother."

But nothing could appease the opponents, not the counsel of Ellen White, not the many obvious accomplishments of the two young educators— not even the tragic death of Ida Magan, which Ellen White had openly attributed to these leaders of the opposition. They wanted to get rid of Sutherland and Magan. When their implacable spirit revealed itself, the two men did as they had planned; they resigned their positions as president and dean of Emmanuel Missionary College.

They did not manifest bitterness or anger as they left their work and the institution which they both loved so much. Although grieved and dismayed, they still knew that they had done right in setting the standards they had for Christian education. They knew that they had followed Ellen White's counsel, and behind them the light of 1888 still focused its beams on their pathway. They were comforted when Mother White told the conference that they were not leaving the college as failures, that they had "acted in harmony with the light God gave. They have worked hard under great difficulties. . . . God has been with them and approved their efforts."

They had laid a permanent basis for the college. By heroic exertion of courage and inspired strength they had overcome many seemingly insurmountable obstacles and were turning out well-educated students who were taking their places in the many fields of service open to them; yet they had alienated an influential portion of the church leaders. Severing connection with the college meant cutting themselves off from denominational employment. Where should they go? What should they do? These two questions spurred them to new exploits in wider fields.

For years both men had been interested in the Southern States still handicapped by the crushing defeat in the War Between the States and the devastated plantations and the breakup of the old customs and traditions that had strangled the South during the years of slavery. On several occasions they had mentioned their interest. Now Mother White suggested that they go south.

Both men still shared the dream of a school where the science of true education might be brought to full fruition, unhampered by criticism—a school where God's plan could be carried out in every particular.

With such a school in mind, Sutherland and Magan went in the spring of 1904 to Nashville and arrived just in time to make the historic trip up the Cumberland River as recorded in the opening chapter of this book.

THE MADISON SCHOOL

Almost two hundred years ago there came to the valley of the Cumberland a band of pioneers from "over on yon side of the mountain." They built crude log cabins and founded a settlement which is now the city of Nashville.

Later another band of pioneers came to the valley of the Cumberland. They also came from "on yon side of the mountain." The visions that guided them were of Christian service, of education for a neglected people. They came, not to build a commonwealth, but a school. The enemies they met were ignorance, poverty, and misunderstanding. The fields that the earlier pioneers had cleared were now worn out and depleted through neglect—fruit of the slave system and aftermath of the war that had impoverished the South.

In an old plantation house, from which the prewar glory had departed, these new pioneers made their home. They had a great leader, Edward Alexander Sutherland, whose name will be linked forever with educational progress and heroic faith in the minds of men both in his home country and beyond the sea. Besides his wife, Sally, he brought a dedicated band: M. Bessie DeGraw; Mrs. Nellie Druillard, who already bore the scars of hard-won battles in many fields; Percy Magan, who would become a world-renowned figure in medical education; and Elmer E. Brink, whose skill in dairy management would probably save their lives.

This band of stalwarts began to build their homes on the Ferguson Farm. They began to till the worn-out soil and to teach. They were destined to toil, to suffer, to sacrifice, and to achieve. When they had established the Madison Center, small groups spread out, not far at first, but near enough to the parent institution to be nourished by counsel and material help. But as time passed they spread farther and farther, until the beneficent influence spread round the world. Newspaper syndicates and other media have told their glorious story. Probably in the annals of educational progress there is not a more unique and inspiring story to relate or to ponder.

Their move to the South, their purchase of the Ferguson Farm, their emphasis on the work-study plan in education—even their intention to conduct self-supporting work—met with disapproval from the leaders in Washington. Even though all the things the two educators were doing had been advised by Ellen White and were in direct line with her counsel, criticism did not cease. The large size of the farm came under criticism. Who would pay for it? The leaders feared that offerings for the new project would drain away funds they deemed necessary for carrying on the regular denominational work, but Sutherland and Magan and their group of loyal followers went forward undaunted. They had the assurance that God approved of their new project, and they had the personal assistance of Ellen White. She counseled with them. She supported them by word and by written articles in the *Review and Herald.* She consented to sit on their board, something she never did for any other institution.

Elder George I. Butler, president of the Southern Union Conference, wanted the new school and was eager for its success. Elder Butler had formerly been General Conference president, and his influence greatly assisted the new venture. Elder S. N. Haskell, who conducted an evangelistic crusade in Nashville that summer of 1904, had always shown himself a friend of Christian education. Also among the supporters of the project were Dr. O. M. Hayward, director of a small sanitarium in Nashville, and Dr. L. C. Isbell, who operated a sanitarium for black people.

The pioneers called the new institution the Madison School. Ellen White had written a series of special testimonies to Madison. She had titled them "The Madison School," and the modest name fitted. Though practical in all its operations, the school organization was somewhat loose and unclassified and altogether unpretentious.

Elders Butler and Haskell, Ellen White, Percy Magan, "Mother" Druillard, M. Bessie DeGraw, and Edward Alexander Sutherland became known as the "rainbow seven" pioneers. They formed the organization known as the Nashville Agricultural and Normal Institute, a holding corporation. Not until 1930 did the school take the name Madison College. The change came about because at that time a branch post office was opened on the campus, and the adjacent village already had a Madison post office.

The "rainbow seven" were also the trustees of Madison School and the N.A.N.I., as the holding corporation was usually referred to. They set to work at once to build and operate a school. Students began to arrive, and by that autumn fourteen had come. Like their teachers they came without thought of money or worldly advantage. What money they could make they could use for living expenses, and their living depended on their making something.

The dean, Percy Magan, gathered up the reins of the mule team and supervised the farm. Miss M. Bessie DeGraw, a secretary, drove to town once a week in a one-mule cart to market the butter which President Sutherland churned and prepared in the lean-to creamery. The treasurer, Mother Druillard, laid her hand to the skillet and the broom. She had few provisions, but she knew how to make the most of what she did have. President Sutherland had embraced Dr. Fletcher's method of thorough mastication, and he almost made the excessive chewing of cornpone a test of fitness.

The farm's chief building, the old plantation house, had been built of cedar logs over a hundred years earlier and later covered with siding and plastered inside. It looked like a typical Southern mansion with a wide veranda. It served as the first schoolroom and meeting place by day and provided

The author, Dr. Ira Gish, right; and coauthor, Elder Harry Christman, left, stand by the memorial erected to the memory of the "rainbow seven" and their work as founders of Madison Collge, the hospital, and affiliated institutions.

sleeping quarters at night until other buildings could be constructed.

The Ferguson family did not give possession of the house until autumn, so those who arrived during the summer had to stay in temporary quarters in the old barn and other outbuildings. Sally Sutherland came in the heat of August with her five-month-old baby boy in her arms. The best shelter available was the servants' quarters in the carriage house above the horse stables. Mrs. Sutherland, Miss Olive Shannon, and Miss Louise Abegg lived in this building for a month and finally dubbed it "Probation Hall," suggesting that anyone who could endure its rigors could qualify for militant participation in whatever Madison had to offer.

"Probation Hall" was hot and overcrowded. Other workers as well lived upstairs. The downstairs quartered servants, mules, horses, and smoked ham, with swarms of rats, mice, and other vermin. How often, during the sweltering August days, Sally Sutherland fanned her baby and turned her eyes to the shady coolness of the deep porches at the plantation house, but not one of the newcomers was allowed to come and sit in the shade, so fierce was the former owner's hatred of those Northerners, "the Yankees."

The yard around the plantation house had pastured calves, colts, geese, and ducks until scarcely a blade of grass showed any spear of green during the dry season. Hogs wallowed just outside the stone fence of the compound, polluting the torrid air with their vile odors and raucous voices. Yet the women in the carriage house did not complain. They had no time. They made the place as clean and neat as possible and went on with their work, singing as they went.

The Fergusons at last vacated the property on the first day of October, and the women moved into the big house. They had little furniture—only a few spring cots and chairs had been purchased—but it was better here than in "Probation Hall." Now, in the evenings, students and faculty gathered round the fireplace, Mother Druillard in the center with her guiding hand on all, her counsel the respected word for young and old. One picture of Mother D persists in the memory of the few remaining pioneers. It portrays her as mistress of the Inn, slaughtering flies morning by morning while they were still stiff from the chilly night. With all her background of affluence, she stood in the forefront of this pioneer movement, taking the jolts as they came. Her courage, her holy trust, and her wise economy helped bring the school through the heavy weather of those early years.

The upstairs apartment in the carriage house was used as a bedroom, and all the pioneers roomed there at one time or another. Then, as relays of students came, they were also quartered in the spare bedroom, and their ability to endure the rough accommodations became something of a test of character. In time the little old weather-beaten carriage house came to be regarded with affection. One can be sure that Sally Sutherland prettied the rooms, cleaned them, and set potted plants around to ornament and freshen the humble place.

The teachers who arrived that summer of 1904 had pooled their resources to buy the land which had cost them $12,723. At the time of its purchase they felt sure that they could raise the money for the balance (after the down payment of $5000). The money was actually due to these teachers from other institutions to whom they had lent it, but now, as the time for payment of the second installment drew near, the teachers discovered that the institutions owing them could not pay without embarrassment. Since they all had a keen interest in these other schools and sanitariums, they could not press for payment. Their source of strength had not failed them before. They went to their knees, and God raised up help. They had founded Madison with the intention of making it a self-supporting venture. They would need donated money not only for buildings and equipment but also for other expenses such as goods and maintenance. They intended to support themselves as efficiently as a farmer supports his family on his own farm. And so they went to work. Edward Sutherland had a magic that somehow transformed the buttermilk and cornpone they ate into something special and delicious. When the family tired of milk toast made of toasted mill-ends, and milk from which every vestige of cream had been removed, someone, for the sake of variety, introduced a new dish called "bruis." The survivors of those times remember this delicacy as toasted mill-ends, in smaller chunks, and the same skim milk.

A dairy herd, a few horses and mules, a flock of chickens and other poultry, and a large drove of hogs came with the property. The hogs did not become Adventist hogs. Mother D sold them herself in the Nashville market and added a substantial amount to a diminishing treasury. For the rest of her life she told the story with many variations.

While the women struggled with high finance and housekeeping on an unbalanced budget, Sutherland and Magan explored new fields of psychology opened to them by the Southern beast of burden, of which Henry the mule was a typical representative.

The dairy herd on the farm proved a substantial source of income. The separated milk and cream were delivered to a cream cellar behind the plantation house, where President Sutherland, with student help, churned the cream into butter which Miss DeGraw took to Nashville in the milk cart and sold to buy sugar, salt, ice, and other necessities. The buttermilk became a major source of nourishment for everyone at the school.

When the diet seemed monotonous, Sutherland reminded everyone of the forty years God rained manna in the wilderness and few complained.

President Sutherland and his fellow founders of Madison had as a prime objective of their effort an institution which would train lay members of the church to join with the organized workers of the denomination and Sutherland's enthusiasm infected everyone around him.

Under their leader's guiding hand, the neglected farm became daily more homelike and more productive. From the beginning Sutherland put into operation the work-study plan which he had introduced at Emmanuel Missionary College. Students and teachers worked together on the farm. Half the day they devoted to study and the other half to labor. Of course money had to be raised for the buildings, machinery, livestock, and improvements; but Edward Sutherland determined that the school would be self-supporting in all the living expenses. They could grow their own food, and already their well-managed dairy provided cash income.

Sutherland and Magan had learned much from Ellen White about the conditions that prevailed in the South—the poverty, ignorance, and great need. Since these men knew that the students could not have an education if they had to pay tuition, no tuition was charged. They had to "work their way" through school, and their teachers helped them in every possible way. An immediate result of this policy was intimate student participation in all the problems of the new school. The day began with morning worship where the whole "family" gathered to sing, to pray, to study God's plans for education, and to discuss great things—great because they involved the deepest longing of every heart in that circle.

Their simple meals were prepared in a large pot. Edward Sutherland, surveying the scene, remembered the schools of the prophets, and his heart thrilled with the possibilities inherent in this little group as they praised God for their simple fare of cornmeal mush or grits and skim milk. Here, in the old plantation house kitchen, breakfasts were a delight.

"Percy," Ed remarked to his beloved friend one day, "our studies must include instruction on how to make a farm pay, how to bring stock through the winter, and how to raise money for all the things we need."

"Do we know how to teach all these subjects?" Percy asked.

Edward Sutherland caught the twinkle in his

eye. "God has promised to supply wisdom, and He will show us how to do it." In the evenings, after the busy day of hard work and study, students and faculty sat basking in the warmth of the north-room fireplace; and Sutherland, looking into the eager faces of the students and their teachers, resolved to make the admonition which Moses commanded Israel in Deuteronomy 6:6, 7 the program for this new institution: "These words . . . shall be in thine heart: and thou shalt teach them diligently unto thy children, and shalt talk of them when thou sittest in thine house, and when thou walkest by the way, and when thou liest down, and when thou risest up."

The matters they discussed around the fireplace varied from folklore and pedagogy to balanced diet, knitting, and how to poultice chapped hands. Yet through all the eager talk ran a thread of dedication to the will of God, and the voice that wove that thread into the conversation was the voice of Edward Sutherland.

That first winter brought hardships. The school had not been in operation long enough for the farm to be brought into production, so not much store of vegetables and fruit had been gathered; but Sutherland envisioned the near future when products of the farm and orchard would furnish them with an adequate and satisfying diet. Good cheer and abounding joy possessed the little company. Everyone felt too hopeful to be discouraged, too busy to be unhappy.

Spring came and planting began. Stones that were scattered all over the neglected farm provided building material, and the students made use of them. Under the guiding hands of their teachers, they built the simple and useful structures that housed the growing institution. Edward Sutherland's keynote and watchword was simplicity. As did George Muller of Bristol, that giant of faith who built the Bristol orphanages in England, Sutherland expected God to supply all their actual needs, but all frills and extras he foreswore as being unnecessary. So firm was his conviction and so great his powers of persuasion that his little group of loyal followers accepted these conditions without complaint, even to the unheated houses.

"Our school must not only give the students preparation for life; it must allow them to experience life." Sutherland spoke as he and Magan walked together across the sprawling campus that spring of 1905. As they often did, they exchanged ideas of whatever concern lay closest to their hearts. "When a student has learned how to make his own living from the land, how to build his house and barn, how to maintain a healthy dairy herd—"

"Yes," Magan interrupted, "and how to handle the everyday problems of farm, school, and church, then he will have an excellence of character stamped on him, wrought within him as a way of life. Then he can go out and start his own little replica of Madison. And that's what you want, isn't it, Ed?"

Edward Sutherland nodded. That was exactly what he wanted.

All competitive sports were discouraged. Madison had no athletic field—no football field or baseball diamond. The farseeing eyes of their leader focused on just the kind of service of which Percy Magan had spoken. The acme of the stu-

113

dents' achievements would be to go out from the parent institution and carve other little self-supporting institutions. So successfully did Edward Sutherland imbue his followers with his ideals that within a short time students of Madison did go out into the needy mountain communities and begin self-supporting work. By the year 1908 a number of them had started their own schools and health centers, and a convention of self-supporting workers convened at Madison to report progress and to share experiences. So much strength and inspiration did they draw from this first meeting that they resolved to hold such a convention every year, and so they do until this day.

Edward Sutherland saw to it that the home base reached out often to the new little schools and health centers. Field trips from Madison brightened many a day for students and workers when they visited Fletcher or Fountain Head (now Highland Academy) or any of the other self-supporting "units" as they came to be called. Like a large and generous family, they considered the basic needs of the smaller members and gave help in every way they could devise. Fostered by such love and care, the units grew and prospered.

And now with the work growing, more cottages and more school buildings had to be built, but more money was needed. Sutherland could not freely solicit funds for his enterprise. The hostility that had begun in Battle Creek years and followed him to Berrien Springs had grown even more widespread since the launching of Madison as a self-supporting institution.

Some leaders feared that Sutherland and Magan would draw off funds from the local conferences which they badly needed to foster their own denominational projects. In some areas Sutherland and Magan were not allowed to solicit any donations. But the counsels of Mother White cheered them. Both men seemed to have a God-given talent for raising funds and influencing men and women of means. They knew that God approved of their project and their work. "If God be for us, who can be against us," they often repeated.

"It is the purpose of this new school to demonstrate to young men and women desirous of doing their Master's service that they can begin a work for Him without the aid of any special equipment, and with only the common buildings to be found on almost any farm."—From a joint article prepared by Sutherland and Magan. *The Invincible Irishman*, p. 62.

STRENGTHENING THE STAKES

The student body had grown to fifteen persons by the spring of 1905, and Sutherland enlisted the students to help in preparing the farm for future fruitfulness. By the middle of March they were setting out apple, peach, pear, and plum trees. They set out a host of loganberry roots and 1800 strawberry plants. Then they planted melons, squash, and other vegetables.

Now Edward Sutherland surveyed the well-tilled acres and the sprouting plants with a special kind of satisfaction. Much remained to be done, but loud and clear he heard the voice behind him saying, "This is the way, walk ye in it."

With prophetic eyes he saw the rolling land covered with blossoming orchard trees and fields of waving corn unfolding silken tresses in the breeze. What though the winter had been so cold and hard;

what though they had subsisted on skim milk and grits? Spring had come, and the promise of God lay like a benediction on the land. With all their hearts both Sutherland and Magan longed to give all their time and strength to the developing project, but money had to be raised.

"Do you think God wants us to solicit funds in our churches, Percy?" Sutherland asked as he straightened his back at the end of a neat row of newly set out strawberry plants. "What scriptural support do we have for doing it. Can't God just send us the money and let us keep on with the work here?"

Percy took off his hat and wiped the sweat from his face and neck with his red bandanna. "I'm sure He could rain money from heaven as easily as He rained manna in the wilderness, but it wouldn't be the best thing."

"You think God's people need to give, need to have their sympathies drawn out to this Southern field?" Sutherland queried.

"Yes, I do, Ed. Do you remember how diligently Paul encouraged the Gentile Christians in the early churches to contribute to the poor saints at Jerusalem?"

Both Sutherland and Magan had ability as speakers, both had peculiar powers of persuasion and magnetic influence. Also they enjoyed raising money for the Lord's work, especially the Lord's needy farm that had been committed to their care along with the group of loyal workers who spent all their time doing the work of developing that farm and that school.

Percy Magan had spent a busy but lonely year since his wife Ida had been laid to rest at the time of the stormy union conference session when he and Edward Sutherland had resigned from Emmanuel Missionary College. But recently he had met a woman doctor who had become important in his life. On a day in early September 1905, Ed Sutherland hitched the mule to the milk cart and drove to the railway station to meet Percy and his new wife, Dr. Lillian. They had been married on August 23 at her home in Cherokee, Iowa.

The coming of Dr. Lillian brought a special talent to the new project. Already a physician in her own right, she could have commanded a good income and ready acceptance at any number of institutions. But she had chosen to cast her lot with this handful of pioneers who struggled with the stern realities of establishing a self-supporting school on the worn-out and neglected acres of the Ferguson Farm.

Edward Sutherland studied Dr. Lillian's reaction to the ride from the railroad station in the mule cart and her facial expression when she was introduced to her new living quarters—an upstairs bedroom in the old plantation house. He could detect nothing but cheerful and willing acceptance of conditions as they were at Madison School in that autumn of 1905.

Actually a lot of hard work had been done, and much had been accomplished. Shortly after Percy Magan and his new wife arrived, Ed and Sally Sutherland with their children, Joe and baby Yolanda, moved into their own modest cottage. Mother Druillard and M. Bessie DeGraw also moved into new cottages at this time. Small functional buildings began to dot the campus, and the gardens and farmland took on a new appearance.

Sutherland, always mindful of Mother White's instruction about sanitarium work being started in connection with our schools, longed for the day when such a development could take place at Madison. In February of 1906 the educators sent a letter to Mother White explaining their prayerful concern for a sanitarium to be started. "It has taken all the strength we have had and all the means we could rake and scrape together to get things going in the school," they explained. "We have had practically no help from the denomination at large and have felt that the burden we have had to carry here was a heavy one."

A foundation principle of the institution, Sutherland always insisted, was self-sacrifice. "Madison should demonstrate the principle of self-support," he added. "If we are to raise up men of the Paul type, we should teach them to become self-supporting workers during the period of student life."

Magan agreed heartily, and the first principle of Madison School's operation became self-support.

One day President Sutherland looked up from his work at a tall young man who had come to apply for entrance. "So you want to attend school here at Madison." He reached out to shake the rough brown hand the youth offered. "Where do you come from?"

"Down Georgia way." A captivating smile crossed the young man's tanned face and lighted his blue eyes. "We heard tell that a man can work hard and go to school here without money."

"That's right, John. Tell me, why do you want to come to Madison to school? I mean, why do you want an education?" President Sutherland asked.

"I know how to plow and plant and milk cows

and slop pigs and all kinds of farm work." The young man from Georgia looked around at the sprawling acres of the Ferguson Farm. "But I do hanker for book-learnin', and I ain't read many books. I do want to understand the Bible."

After satisfying himself that this youth had a genuine wish to learn in order to serve his community and his God better, Sutherland said, "You need to take some review classes in reading, writing, and arithmetic; but you will soon go on to advanced work. I know you will learn fast." Then he explained the work-study plan and assured John that he would be able to work enough to pay for his tuition, his room, board, and laundry, and also that he would be expected to work two hours each working day to help pay the operating expenses of the school.

Other students came, young people who could never have an education unless Madison made it possible. Sutherland, looking at them, talking with them, working with them, came to love them in a special way.

The matter of support for the faculty came up for discussion, and by mutual agreement the instructors allowed themselves a salary of thirteen dollars a month. In 1908, when Madison had entered its fourth year, the teachers were credited with thirteen dollars a month and were charged with board, room, laundry, livery hire, etc. At the end of the year the profit the school had earned was divided into three parts. One part was divided among the teachers; it figured out at twelve cents an hour for their time. The other two thirds went for repairs, improvement, and expansion.

In 1918 the teachers were still drawing the same

amount of salary—thirteen dollars a month. President Sutherland received a special thrill when a committee action that year was laid before him:

"Voted on motion of Mrs. Druillard, seconded by Miss DeGraw to put on record the opinion of the faculty and the Board, that while it has been impossible for the faculty to receive a higher wage, each member feels more than repaid for the effort he has devoted to this work, and is devoutly thankful for the progress which God's blessing has made possible."

There were people who questioned whether Professor Magan and President Sutherland actually lived on thirteen dollars a month. Professor Magan clarified this matter at a meeting of the patrons in 1912. He said that neither he nor President Sutherland had ever made a statement that they lived on thirteen dollars a month. They did declare that all they ever drew from Madison School was thirteen dollars a month. Because of their greater responsibility for traveling, fund-raising, etc., they needed more and had to have money from other "sources." Both men had some income from family property holdings which they used.

Sutherland early enunciated a second basic principle of Madison's operation—a strict and persistent economy. As the school grew and new buildings were planned, he decided against large, expensive, modern, and well-equipped buildings. If such were erected, would not the graduate of Madison expect the same kind of facilities in starting new work? He decided, and his followers agreed, that the new buildings would need to be small, simple, and inexpensive and that students and teachers should work together in building them, thus learning how to erect such buildings as would suit them best in their after work. So Madison adopted the cottage plan of housing students. Later, however, the institution did erect larger buildings and finally two dormitories.

The school followed a "One Study Plan," and it became the third basic principle at Madison. The students carried just one major subject. They gave three hours a day to classwork in that subject and three more hours to preparation for class. During one term the student covered in succession as much work as if three or more major studies were taken simultaneously. Through the remaining hours of the day the work program gave them both training and practice in the industrial department. The student was changed from one line of work to another until he received a well-rounded training in the care and management of livestock and poultry, garden and dairy, the building program, as well as development of the farm and its varied crops.

The fourth and last basic principle which President Sutherland felt contributed much to the stability of Madison School was self-government. Early in the first year he called a meeting of students and teachers with the purpose of developing true Christian democracy. This group, known as the Union Body, became the legislative force in the school with the executive power.

Sutherland read the instructions from Mother White: "The rules governing the schoolroom should, so far as possible represent the voice of the school. Every principle involved must be set so clearly before the student that he may be convinced of its justice. Thus, he will feel a responsibility to see that the rules he himself has helped to frame shall be enforced."

Both faculty and student body recognized the wisdom of this instruction, and the Union Body with its meetings became one of the strongest single educational features of the school.

Under these four basic principles President Sutherland saw the Madison School grow and prosper. The passing months brought steady development and healthy expansion. Gone now were the old hogpens that had blemished the front yards and defiled the view from the windows of the plantation house. Already many stones had been removed from the land, and the soil was being built up by every means that President Sutherland and Percy Magan could devise.

They sorely needed a school building. They prayed many times, most earnestly; but the money did not come.

One day after a heart-searching season of prayer over this matter, Percy said, "Ed, I think maybe God has a special purpose in limiting us to the old plantation house. Perhaps He intends that this hardship shall be an example to the other students who go out to start their own self-supporting centers."

"Do you think we should slack off our praying about the school building?" Ed asked.

"No, indeed. We should double our prayers. God will send us the money for the building at the right time."

So the plantation house served as a school building and assembly hall by day, and by night it provided sleeping quarters.

In spite of hard work, both physical and mental—

in spite of criticism that assailed him from high places—those early years at Madison were happy years for Edward Sutherland. His home rejoiced with the laughter of little children and their merry-hearted mother. His students grew daily more responsive to his instruction, and his loyal band of fellow workers gave him all their strength and support. But one thing troubled him. He had not yet been able to start the sanitarium. There seemed no way to extend themselves further.

"To the workers in Madison I would say, Be of good courage. Do not lose faith. Your heavenly Father has not left you to achieve success by your own endeavors. Trust in Him, and He will work in your behalf."—*Special Testimonies*, Series B, no. 11, p. 17.

HEALTH EVANGELISM JOINED TO EDUCATIONAL PROGRESS

From the earliest days at Madison President Sutherland had envisioned a union of school and sanitarium. The instruction received from Mother White insisted on it: "It is essential that there shall be a sanitarium connected with the Madison School. The educational work at the school and the sanitarium can go forward hand in hand."

In February of 1906 a report of the school went to Mother White describing the program in use to train missionary workers: "We teach them the Bible, physiology and hygiene, the English language, church history, the keeping of accounts, and how to give simple treatments. . . . We are planning that no girl shall leave our school who is not a good cook, and able to make her own clothes, and do simple nursing."

The intention to foster the medical work already

existed, but neither Sutherland nor Magan could yet see their way clear to build a sanitarium. Would people from Nashville come out there for medical treatment? The road from the main highway was narrow—almost impassable for part of the year. Sutherland had no experience in running a medical institution, and he knew that Magan hadn't either. They had no money to build even the school buildings they so desperately needed. How could they even consider starting a sanitarium? The whole thing seemed as impossible as Madison School had seemed two years before from that rock pile by the old barn.

Then, one day, Mother White paid a visit to Madison. Edward Sutherland saw with a catch at his heart that the years had laid their weight on Mother White. In her honor the faculty and students arranged a picnic, and while they all sat eating lunch on a beautiful wooded slope just west of the school buildings, she suddenly spoke out. "This would be a good spot for a sanitarium."

No one answered her. Silence fell on them all, but they had heard the words. Mother White's voice still retained its remarkable carrying power. The picnickers continued to pass the food and pour the lemonade. Then Mother White spoke again, "You say you have no money, but you need to have faith." She looked around at them all, and each one seemed to feel the weight of that look. "Do you have faith anymore? Get your people together, and get a horse and mark out the site, even though you don't have money to begin."

The words fell like an electric shock on the small company. But when they had finished their picnic lunch, they hurried to their little chapel and knelt in prayer. Then they got a mule, hitched him to a plow and marked out the spot where the sanitarium would be built.

Mother White went back to California. But, one way or another, the good Lord, who directed all the affairs at Madison, planned to get that sanitarium opened.

Sometime later a tired and ailing businessman from Nashville came to the Madison campus. "I have heard that you folk give treatment for the sick and furnish them a healthful diet. Will you let me come here and try to get well?"

The women looked at him in consternation. "We are not quite ready to do that yet," Mother Druillard explained.

The man could not be turned aside so easily, and finally Mother D screened off a corner of the plantation house porch to provide temporary quarters for this first patient; and with her usual determination, wisdom, and skill she and her three nursing students ministered so successfully to this guest that he recovered his health and went back to Nashville to spread the good news.

The first building for the sanitarium, a small cottage with a capacity for eleven beds, contained treatment rooms opening onto a porch. Kerosene lamps lighted it, and a wood stove heated it and boiled the water for hydrotherapy treatments. A wide board on two wooden sawhorses provided a treatment table, yet to this humble institution came the elite of Nashville. Here they found healing for both bodies and souls, for the workers demonstrated supreme efficiency and a Christlike kindness which inspired confidence and hope.

The year 1907 proved to be an especially hard one for the infant institution. President Sutherland saw the alfalfa crop drown in the cold wet spring. It was necessary to replant the corn, killed by the same weather. Then the intense heat of summer, together with a drought, dried up the sorghum crop. Garden vegetables withered, and even the potatoes refused to develop. Pumping water for the stock became a long and difficult job.

Added to concern for the farm came continuing criticism from church leaders. That autumn President Sutherland had to leave the campus. He had become so weary in body and mind that he surrendered all affairs of the school and sanitarium into the hands of his trusted co-workers. He rested for several weeks and encouraged himself in the Lord who had never failed him.

Percy Magan, with loyal faculty members and faithful students, kept the farm running. Mother D, past sixty years of age, took hold of the sanitarium work in her usual vigorous way. Her methods might be described as a mixture of hydrotherapy, gumption, and the fear of God. With the three nurses she had been training, she met every situation and made the maximum use of the facilities at hand.

When President Sutherland was able, he went to the West Coast to raise money, while Magan and his helpers worked on the sanitarium building.

When the new building was completed, Dr. Lillian, who had been working at a sanitarium in Nashville, became the first physician to connect with the Madison Sanitarium. Dr. Newton Evans joined Dr. Lillian and became the first medical superintendent of the institution.

Mother White, sensitive to the needs of the growing work all over the world, had still a special care for Madison and its leaders, Edward Sutherland and Percy Magan. In 1907 she wrote to the General Conference leaders: "You have a work to do to encourage the school work in Madison, Tennessee. . . . The workers who have been striving to carry out the mind and will of God in Madison have not received the encouragement they should have. . . . The brethren who have influence should do all in their power to hold up the hands of these workers by encouraging and supporting the work of the Madison school. Means should be appropriated to the needs of the work in Madison, that the labor of the teachers may not be so hard in the future."

At the Southern Union Conference session held in Nashville in January 1908, Elder A. G. Daniells, president of the General Conference, and Frederick Griggs and other church leaders took an objective look at Madison and its development, and the conference gave it a vote of confidence. Elder Daniells called for a spirit of unity and assured Sutherland and Magan that the institutions would continue "in the favor of the denomination." The conference appropriated $19,500 to the Madison School, bringing a special thrill of joy to Sutherland and Magan and new courage to the faculty and students.

That same winter of 1908 a smallpox epidemic struck the student body at the school. Dr. Lillian called the county health officer, who promptly quarantined the student body. This first contact with Nashville physicians proved to be a boon to the fledgling sanitarium. Also, Dr. Lillian, with the help of two nurses, brought eight cases of the dreadful disease through without the loss of one. The health officer, watching the situation closely, did not fail to recognize the skill and quality of service rendered. Neither did he fail to talk about it, and his friends listened.

Now the sanitarium work grew with a rapidity that astonished even those closest to it. Even now it was beginning to add substantially to the income. Cottage after cottage provided more and more room for expansion. From its small beginnings in an eleven-bed cottage it was already making giant strides toward the large and important institution it would shortly become. President Sutherland thought often of the prophetic words Mother White had spoken.

The year 1910 rolled around. Sutherland felt that the worst of Madison's "growing pains" were over. The sanitarium prospered greatly under the administration of Drs. Newton Evans and Lillian Magan. The Madison School had made great advances in the six years since its founding. With all the responsibility devolving upon them and with the future expanding at a dramatic rate in front of their far-seeing eyes, Sutherland and Magan began to think seriously of some advice that Dr. Kellogg had given them years earlier at Battle Creek. "You both ought to take the medical course. Whichever way you turn, whatever you decide to do, the medical course will be an advantage to you," he had said.

Several times Edward Sutherland had set his mind to follow Dr. Kellogg's advice, but other weighty matters had diverted him. Magan did not seem interested. Now Sutherland decided to attend classes at the medical school in Nashville. Magan decided to take medicine as well. The two life-long friends enrolled together in the autumn of 1910. They still lived on the Madison campus and commuted back and forth on motorcycles.

Sutherland began to see more clearly how much training would mean to his future work at Madison. When an urgent call came from Loma Linda, California, for Dr. Evans to join the staff at the fledgling medical school there, Sutherland felt depressed, but what relief to him when Dr. Evans refused to leave unless a qualified doctor could be found to replace him.

This refusal of the call did not settle the matter though. The call for Dr. Evans came again with great urgency. Conditions at the College of Medical Evangelists became so serious that even President Sutherland agreed that Dr. Evans must go, but how would they manage without him? The two leaders, Sutherland and Magan, still lacked three years of finishing their four-year course. The consensus of opinion among the faculty as well as the sanitarium staff strongly advised that Sutherland and Magan continue with their medical training, and they hastened to rise to the emergency. They decided that Dr. Lillian Magan should take charge of the sanitarium and its patients. Mother Druillard would be superintendent of the institution and its business manager. Miss DeGraw would head the school. They chose Mr. Rocke to direct the agricultural work and manage the industries.

Heartened by this display of loyalty and devotion, grateful also that by their sacrifice they might assist the new medical school in the West, Sutherland and Magan went forward with fresh vigor. The work at Madison grew and prospered, for the Lord worked with them. Three years later the two men both returned to responsibilities on the campus as physicians.

The bond of fellowship between them had strengthened, and now they felt sure that nothing would ever part them. Dr. Sutherland remembered how he and Percy had accepted righteousness by faith and had sat at Mother White's feet learning the meaning of that message. Together they had felt the urge for reform at Battle Creek. Together they had moved Battle Creek College to Berrien Springs, Michigan, and had fought out the battle for "the true science of education." Together they had solicited funds for the infant college, and together they had resigned in the spring of 1904. Together they had wept on the rock near the old plantation house on the rocky and neglected Ferguson Farm in the hour of their Gethsemane. Together they had expended every power of their bodies and minds to make the run-down acres into the "Beautiful Farm" that Mother White had envisioned. Together they had entered the medical course when they were no longer young men. They had completed it together, and now they stood on an elevation where they could look forward to a bright future for Madison.

Then, in the summer of 1914 a distinguished visitor appeared on Madison campus, Elder E. E. Andross, president of the board of the College of Medical Evangelists. He had brought Dr. Newton Evans with him, and he had come to urge Percy Magan to join the faculty of the new institution. Dr. Sutherland felt as though he could not endure such a separation; yet he left Magan free to make his own decision. It was a decided refusal, and Sutherland and the Madison family breathed a great sigh of relief.

Later that same autumn, Elder W. C. White sent a letter to Magan urging him to "join the Loma Linda faculty and take leadership of the work in Los Angeles."

Dr. Magan in his deepest self did not want to go west, but under the combined persuasion of the church leaders, he did leave the school he loved so dearly, and he never returned except for short visits. Dr. Sutherland felt his loss. "This is like tearing asunder bone and marrow," he said out of his deep grief over the final decision.

Yet even in this hour of tremendous sacrifice, he could say, "This may be an opportunity for both of us to do more in strengthening right principles of education, both in medical lines and in regular school work."

He looked back some thirty years to the time when he and Percy had met at Battle Creek. He believed that God had led them both to this present hour and was even now working out something of value through their united efforts. "I believe that God has ways and means of holding through the hard places." He tried to comfort the ones who shared his loss—the workers and students. "If we will stand still," he said, "and have confidence that the One who has brought us to this point is telling us to go forward, He will provide facilities." Then he recalled such places in his own life experience where God had worked just such wonders of guidance and fulfillment.

So Dr. Magan and his family moved west to

Loma Linda, and the school and sanitarium which he and Sutherland had done so much to found and establish missed him more than anyone could express. But they closed ranks and from that day they felt that they had an outpost in California. The interests of the struggling medical school somehow became their own. They had made a heavy investment in the College of Medical Evangelists.

> **Madison's aim is the training not of mere teachers of abstract sciences, but of teachers of the art of living. At this school the effort is made to give the student, not merely a preparation for life, but an experience in life.**—A. W. Spalding, *Men of the Mountains*, pp. 160, 161.

WITH UNDIMINISHED FAITH

Dr. Edward Alexander Sutherland faced the future of Madison's twin institutions with the same calm assurance that had carried him through its first decade. He looked around him and saw the once despised Ferguson Farm, already under remedial soil treatment, now bringing forth an abundance of varied crops. Although his lifetime friend and fellow builder had gone to join the faculty of the medical college in Loma Linda, he knew that the God he served remained.

Sutherland looked with satisfaction upon the flourishing school with its loyal teachers and faithful students. He considered the young sanitarium with its growing patronage and its skillful nurses and directors. His vision took in the "units," little replicas of Madison, that had already sprung up throughout the Southland. Their yearly convocation brought 250 self-supporting workers back to the home campus every year with stories of the miracle-working power of God and victories of faith. Dr. Sutherland missed Percy Magan more than he could explain to anyone, but his faith in the future did not falter; he encouraged himself in the Lord and pressed forward with renewed determination.

Before long he began to receive letters from the West informing him of the great needs and the enormous problems of the new medical school. In order to upgrade the quality of education offered by the College of Medical Evangelists, the board had voted to establish a division of the college in Los Angeles. For this purpose $60,000 would be needed at once. Percy wrote that the General Conference could see no way to raise so much money, and many of the board members favored closing the school.

Dr. Sutherland acted at once. First he called on Mrs. S. N. Haskell, who lived in Nashville. He also called upon Mrs. Josephine Gotzian, who lived on the Madison campus. Dr. Sutherland had lived in her home in St. Paul, Minnesota, while he had been canvassing one summer. She had become an Adventist shortly before because of the influence of the folk at Battle Creek Sanitarium where she had been a patient. He explained to the two women the problems Percy Magan faced in his new post as dean of the medical school in California.

"I would like you women to go to California and team up with Emma Gray and Dr. Florence Keller," Sutherland said. "Please go in the name and power of God and do what you can do to save the medical school."

Later Percy Magan wrote of the dramatic occurrence. The College of Medical Evangelists Board had met to close the school. Opposition to continuance of the program had grown too strong. The men had begun their discussion when a gentle tap sounded on the door. Someone opened it.

Four women entered the room. In earnest tones they pleaded with the board to continue the medical school. They asked that the teaching unit be built in Los Angeles, that it be dedicated and made sacred to the memory of Ellen G. White, and that the task of raising money for this undertaking be committed to the women of the church.

A hush filled the room. The board members listened and gave their approval. Then these quiet messengers of hope, none of whom held any official position in the church they loved, withdrew; but their words had reversed the trend toward doubt and failure and inspired courage in many hearts.

"I knew that you had sent them, Ed," Percy wrote in his letter of thanksgiving, "but I didn't breathe a word to anyone present."

This action, prompted by the generous heart of Dr. Sutherland, marked the beginning of Madison's aid to the medical school. Mrs. Lida Scott, a member of the Madison faculty and one of its board of directors, had promised to give a substantial gift to the Madison Institution. Now, with the approval of Madison's founders, and in answer to Percy Magan's request for help, she gave $30,000. Later the Madison group increased this amount to $50,000. Such was the splendid dowry that Madison bestowed on the College of Medical Evangelists.

Not only did Madison give money, but they gave a more precious boon—men and women: Dr. Newton Evans, Dr. Percy Magan, Martha Berger, who served as director of nurses at the White Memorial Hospital for a number of years, and O. R. Staines—all from Madison.

This generous giving of their means, men, and women gave Edward Sutherland genuine comfort. He had not only envisioned God's larger plan, but he and all his staff were participating in the new medical development in the West. Years later he explained how the work in the South had benefitted. "This union has more sanitariums than any other union conference in the world," he told a convention of self-supporting workers. "This came about through cooperation between Madison's medical department and the graduates of C.M.E." The college in the West did not forget its benefactors, and many of the graduates chose to set up their medical practices in the South where they might spread Madison's ideals and inspiration.

From his youth as a young professor at Battle Creek College, Dr. Sutherland had concerned himself with the subject of nutrition. He had listened to Mother White's instructions and accepted a meatless diet as part of his way of thinking and living. He had introduced a vegetarian diet at the beginning of Walla Walla College and made it the first of our educational institutions to serve a strictly non-meat diet. When he went back to Battle Creek and later at Berrien Springs he continued the practice, and he established a similar program at Madison. But he felt that he must do more.

He recalled that Mother White had said: "It

would be a great advantage to the school at Madison if a food factory were put into operation in connection with the work of the school."

At another time she had said: "The health food business is one of the Lord's own instrumentalities to supply a necessity."

And still another time she had written: "As God gave manna from heaven to sustain the children of Israel, so He will now give His people in different places skill and wisdom to use the products of these countries in preparing food to take the place of meat."

Shortly after the establishment of a school at Madison, a large health-food factory opened at Edgefield, only a few miles from Madison. But it did not prosper because the people of the South had not been educated or conditioned to enjoy health foods. They preferred their corn pone and bacon. So the health-food factory became a "white elephant" in the hands of its owners. It passed from hand to hand with no success. Then came the final decision to dismantle the plant. But the hand of God had hovered over that equipment and over the mind of Dr. Sutherland. He had kept watch over the fortunes of the failing health-food company, and many times he had longed to open such a factory at Madison but had always felt that without essential know-how and without money for the project they could surely not expect to succeed where skilled heads and hands had failed.

But now Edward Sutherland felt impressed to purchase the plant. He took the matter to his faculty. How could they learn to prepare attractive meatless foods? How could they market their product? How could they raise the necessary money?

Then Dr. Sutherland read a statement from Mother White: "The heavenly Provider of all foods will not leave His people in ignorance in regard to the preparation of the best foods for all times and all occasions."

He closed the book and looked around at them all. "These are our orders." A smile lighted his far-seeing blue eyes. "With faith and work, we can make a success of the business and the Lord will teach us how to prepare these foods."

The faculty approved the plan and purchased the equipment. A new industry had been added to the school plant. A number of years had passed since the first message from Mother White had begun to agitate Edward Sutherland's mind.

Sutherland intended to begin small, training workers step by step. That dynamo of resourcefulness, Mother Nellie Druillard, took on the direction of the food factory; and under God's blessing it prospered. It achieved phenomenal growth and success. Before long Sutherland could say, "Our products are found in all the states, in Canada, and in foreign lands."

The founder of Madison had one fundamental purpose—to train young men and women for self-supporting work. He held it always before them, as the ideal of service. He repeated often the words of Mother White: "Every possible means should be devised to establish schools after the Madison order."

One day two of the first students came to him, Charles Alden and Bradford Mulford. "We haven't been here very long," Charles said, "but do you think we know enough to go and start a school in the hills?"

Sutherland felt a thrill of bounding joy. "You know how to build your house and your school?"

"Yes, we know how to use stones like we have here, and we can use logs too."

"You know how to handle animals, mules, cattle?"

"We do it all the time here."

So Sutherland encouraged the two young men to go out in the hills and start their own self-supporting school and gospel ministry. Later he went to visit them and heard an old mountain man describe their program. "They he'p the 'pore.' They he'p the sick. They 'larn' our children, and they hold Sunday School."

Edward Alexander Sutherland knew that this little offshoot of Madison would succeed, and his heart rejoiced, because he could foresee many other young people opening many other centers of light throughout the southland.

Then another married student, Calvin Kinsman, came to him and proposed a plan of establishing a center like Madison in Cuba. Calvin, his wife, and Oren Wolcott, a friend, wanted to go to Cuba.

"You attended Emmanuel Missionary College, didn't you?" Sutherland asked Kinsman.

"Yes, we did, and we came here to Madison at the beginning."

"Yes, I remember that you lived in 'Probation Hall' and know all about its hardships and inconveniences." Dr. Sutherland searched their eager young faces. "Have you any money to buy land and equipment?"

"We have enough to land us in Cuba and a little more to live on. We expect to work while we learn Spanish," Kinsman answered, and his wife and friend nodded in agreement.

Sutherland recalled how these young men had helped plant the first gardens on the neglected Ferguson Farm. They had helped build the first cottages. They had worked for their meals. Yes, with God's blessing, they would do well in Cuba. Without hesitation he gave them his blessing, and they did go to Cuba. With the help of friends they purchased land and opened a school, and for a number of years they served God in Cuba.

So strong was the motivation for establishing "units," as they came to be called, that many sprang into active life during the early years of Madison's career. At one time as many as fifty such schools functioned in seven of the Southern States. Some grew into rather large schools and hospitals. Others remained small. Some served for a time and served their purpose, or were taken over by the local conferences. One was the former Fountain Head School and Sanitarium, now Highland Academy.

Dr. Sutherland contemplated these "units" with a great deal of satisfaction. "As a parent rejoices in the accomplishments of his children, so Madison College feels a pardonable pride . . . in the good work done by the small institutions."

The young and dedicated Christian students who went out and carved these small centers out of the hilly forests manifested heroic faith and made incredible sacrifices. Edward Sutherland bore the burden of their need always on his heart and mind. He prayed for them. He talked for them. And God sent him help.

Mrs. Lida Scott, a daughter of Mr. Funk of Funk and Wagnalls Publishing Company, first came in contact with Seventh-day Adventists at Battle Creek Sanitarium, where their methods of healthful living and their Christian attitudes attracted her. She heard of the work that Sutherland and Magan had started in the Southland. In 1914 she visited Madison. What she saw impressed her so much that she joined the organization, and her name is listed among the "Rainbow Seven" pioneers.

This woman, reared in a wealthy home and surrounded by luxury from early childhood, embraced the life on Madison campus and the ideals and aim of its founders with her whole heart. Her inheritance from her father's publishing interests made her a wealthy woman in her own right. Just before coming to Madison she lost her only child. During all the years that Lida Scott lived on Madison campus, scarcely a day passed that she did not mention that lovely daughter who had been the light of her life.

Not long after she had joined the Madison School, someone said to her, "You came to Madison because you were ill, and I suppose you stayed because they saved your life."

"No, that is not the reason I remained." Mrs. Scott flashed one of her rare smiles. "I remained because they showed me that my life was worth living."

By 1914 the twin institutions at Madison had become so large that they took the entire time and strength of the whole faculty. Someone must give attention to the extension work and the many "units." Who can doubt that God sent Lida Scott to the sanitarium and that He touched her heart. She became interested in the work of the "units." She gave money with inspired generosity; but most important, she gave herself. She visited the most remote locations where she worked under conditions so crude and difficult that they would have discouraged a less dedicated spirit. Edward Sutherland watched with awe and holy joy while Mrs. Scott changed the whole character of the layman's movement in the "units." He saw her bring them up to higher standards and infuse them with her own inspiration.

In 1924, ten years after Mrs. Scott settled in Madison and twenty years before her death, she assigned her fortune to a fund which would promote the Madison idea of education in the "units" as well as the mother institution. Thus the Layman Foundation, a non-profit organization, incorporated under the Welfare Act of the State of Tennessee, became a vital reality. The five incorporators were Dr. E. A. Sutherland, president; Lida Funk Scott, treasurer; M. Bessie DeGraw; Mrs. N. H. Druillard; and W. F. Rocke. To this organization Mrs. Scott transferred her entire fortune of more than a million dollars. At her death she left only her modest home, a personal estate of less than one thousand dollars.

The Layman Foundation had one purpose— founding and fostering self-supporting work. It gave or lent money to the small institutions which were the offspring of Madison School.

During her first ten years at Madison, Mrs. Scott had given many thousands of dollars to the school plant. The demonstration school building, the science building (Bralliar Hall), and the Helen Funk Assembly Hall were all gifts from Mrs. Scott.

Dr. Sutherland felt that he owed much to this

godly woman who had now dedicated the whole of her remaining fortune to the Layman Foundation. He regarded her as the mother of this important organization. He had suffered much opposition from those who should have been his friends, but God had given him favor with others who dedicated their money, their talents, and their devoted loyalty to the projects he fostered.

His aunt, Mrs. Nellie Druillard, had been with him from the beginning of the Madison project; and the years of responsible service she rendered had a value that he recognized as beyond computation in money. She also gave of her means toward the construction of many projects. She left her estate of between twenty-five and thirty thousand dollars to the Rural Education Association to be administered by Dr. E. A. Sutherland.

Mrs. Josephine Gotzian, whom Sutherland met in his youth, became a much-appreciated benefactor of Madison. She gave the money for Gotzian Hall and Gotzian Health Home, originally built for treatment rooms and devoted to the care of the sick among the institutional family. It later became Gotzian Home and Nurses' Dormitory.

So much favor did God grant this man of faith and vision that gifts of money came in for farm equipment, for buildings, and for the establishment of new industries that his dream of a self-supporting institution came true before his eyes. More than that, God surrounded him with a staff of workers whose loyalty and devotion could not be shaken by all manner of hardship or by any outside allurement.

M. Bessie DeGraw had been with him as a staunch supporter since the early days at Walla

Walla. Her many talents and her finest efforts she expended in glad service every day of her life; and she, like the others, drew only thirteen dollars a month from Madison School.

Nearer and dearer than all, Sally, his wife, with her gentle leadership and endearing ways, not only brightened his home and mothered his two children, but she took an active part in the affairs of the institution. Her merry laughter rang out over many a dark day, and her ready sympathy and understanding endeared her to students and workers alike.

> "Wicked men and devils cannot hinder the work of God, or shut out His presence from the assemblies of His people, if they will, with subdued, contrite hearts, confess and put away their sins, and in faith claim His promises."—*Selected Messages*, bk. 1, p. 124.

GOD'S PLAN UNFOLDS

One summer day in 1915 Yolanda Sutherland brought the mail to her father. He laid it out on the table in their cottage. First he tore the wrapper off the *Review and Herald* and spread the paper flat on the table.

"Come, Sally, and look at this!" he gasped.

Across the front cover of the paper a big black banner announced the death of Ellen G. White. They stood looking at it, their hearts swelling with grief for their great loss, but glad that they had known Mother White so long and so well. Edward Alexander Sutherland recalled that year of 1888 when he and Percy Magan had sat at Mother White's feet and shared her delight in the message of righteousness by faith. During the twenty-seven years that had passed since then his close friendship with Mother White had grown into unquestioning confidence that God had indeed chosen this woman to communicate His messages to His people. He knew that the project at Madison could never have been launched and could never have survived without the encouragement Mother White had given them. He and his loyal staff of workers could never have survived the severe and repeated criticism that had harrassed them from the beginning.

Sally broke into his reverie, "Do you remember that time when she sent us the message 'to the workers in Madison I would say, Be of good courage. Do not lose faith. Your heavenly Father has not left you to achieve success by your own endeavors. Trust in Him and He will work in your behalf' "?

"You must have memorized that one." He gave Sally a tender smile.

"Yes, and I memorized several others. I repeat them often to myself. They always renew my courage."

Dr. Sutherland smoothed the *Review* lying on the table and opened it to the obituary. They read it together.

All the rest of that day the precious words of encouragement Mother White had written about the work at Madison kept crowding into Dr. Sutherland's mind. He remembered also predictions she had made that even now seemed impossible of fulfillment, such as that one about Madison School being a "spectacle to the world."

War had already broken out in Europe and pressure mounted daily for the United States to enter the conflict. If war did come to this country, what

148

effect would it have on Madison School and Sanitarium?

In 1917 the Southern Accrediting Association accepted the Madison High School into its association. It had been offering work of a quality acceptable as entrance requirements for the College of Medical Evangelists.

In April of 1917 the United States entered the war as an ally of France and the other countries struggling to drive back the aggressors. Madison School, now thirteen years old, braced herself for the hardships that would surely follow. Food rationing troubled Madison's people less than it troubled most others. They already knew how to conserve food, and the abstemiousness of the war years changed their pattern of diet and work very little; but the draft took away students as well as several teachers and other key workers. Those who remained carried on and prayed for the war to end. So well did they discharge their duties that before the war ended in 1918, Madison School had expanded to junior college level. In 1923 the management took the first steps toward recognition as a junior college and achieved that status in 1928, when the Southern Association of College and Secondary Schools gave accreditation to Madison Junior College.

So much did the Lord prosper this outstanding experiment in education that its growth demanded a new form of management. So Dr. Sutherland and his associates formed a new corporation, *The Rural Educational Association,* which began operation of the school on June 1, 1924. The original corporation, N.A.N.I., continued to hold title to the real estate.

God endowed Edward Sutherland with wisdom in business management that enabled him to expand and develop the twin institutions, Madison Sanitarium and Madison School. At the same time he fortified every such expansion with the support needed to maintain healthy growth. God also gave him such favor with his associates that he enjoyed a measure of loyalty and childlike trust from them that contributed much to the success of his undertakings. Several of those who joined him in the Madison School project at its beginning stayed on to give all the remaining years of their lives to the man and the institutions they had come to love. They knew that God directed him, and they felt secure.

In 1930 Dr. Sutherland set in motion plans to make Madison a senior college, and in November of 1933 the Tennessee College Association officially accepted it as a senior college.

So the little school born of adversity and faith had grown into a senior college, and one outstanding characteristic made it unique among colleges— it was self-supporting. Now it stood ready to be discovered by the world, for Ellen White had predicted that it would be a "spectacle to the world, to angels, and to men."

> "Oh how great is thy goodness, which thou hast laid up for them that fear Thee; which thou hast wrought for them that trust in Thee before the sons of men!—
> Psalm 31:19.

WORLD RESPONSE

Between the years 1930 to 1950, Madison enjoyed a "golden age." Newspapers brought attention to the self-supporting institution that was seeking senior college status. The Nashville *Banner* carried a half page of pictures and explanatory text on the aim and purpose of the school. An editorial appeared in *The Nation's Commerce*, dated September 15, 1934. The article that brought the most favorable and lasting publicity to Madison appeared in the May 1938 issue of *Reader's Digest*. The article by Weldon Melick, entitled "Self-Supporting College," brought nearly five thousand applications to Madison and sparked over twenty thousand letters of inquiry. The article explained the principles on which the school operated in most laudatory terms. Immediate and dramatic results followed. Applications poured in from India, Africa, Turkey, China, Russia—from everywhere. Ripley's *Believe It or Not* carried an article in its South American edition about the Madison School.

The following year enrollment reached the highest point in Madison's history with nearly 500 registrations.

In June of 1938 the New York *Times* sent a photographer and a reporter to the campus to capture the spirit of the place in story and pictures. Newspapers all over the United States followed with feature articles. On October 7 of that same year Eleanor Roosevelt presented Madison in glowing terms in her syndicated column, *My Day*. She reported an interview she had arranged with Madison's Dr. Floyd Bralliar, brother-in-law of Dr. Sutherland, at the special request of Secretary of State Cordell Hull.

Late in 1938 the Roman Catholic periodical *The Commonwealth* sent a man to Madison to spend several days studying the school and the principles on which it operated. He wrote an article charged with emotion which appeared in the issue of January 8, 1939. In it he held up Madison and its work and its influence around the world as a challenge to his church. He urged his people to recognize the "golden opportunity" held out to them by the Madison plan.

One month later in his *Believe It or Not* Ripley displayed a sketch of Madison's Druillard Library with a brief statement about the unusual nature of Madison College. He labeled it, "the only self-supporting college in America."

A year later *Coronet,* in its January 1, 1940, issue, started its section "A Portfolio of Personalities" with a brief sketch of Dr. E. A. Sutherland's work as founder of Madison College. On the opposite page it displayed a full-page picture of him.

And what of the man who had already spent over thirty-five years of his life fostering and building the twin institutions on the farm he had considered so hopeless? Among all the plaudits of public acclaim touched now by the spotlight of world approval, how did the man react? He looked about him and saw the quiet prophecies of Mother White blossoming into a fulfillment he and Percy Magan could never have imagined in 1904 when they wept on the old rock pile and prayed, as Christ had done in Gethsemane, to be delivered from the bitter cup. Yet their choice in that hour of agony had been, "Thy will, not mine, be done." They had staked everything on the revelations of God to Mother White.

They had experienced privation, tribulation, persecution from those who should have sustained them; and through it all this man, Edward Alexander Sutherland, had been obedient to the heavenly vision of a "Beautiful Farm." Having put his hand to the plow, he refused to turn back or to swerve to the right hand or the left. Now he saw one of the most unlikely of Mother White's prophecies unfolding around him and bursting into unexpected dimensions. She had said that the work at Madison would become "a spectacle to the world, to angels, and to men."

In Dr. Sutherland's thinking and planning this farm had become a dedicated demonstration of what God can do with common men when they follow His directions with a vigorous purpose. No matter what had happened in the past, no matter what the future might hold, nothing could alter the glorious fact that during the first half of the twentieth century God had done a unique, a miraculous, thing on planet Earth. He had done it with a handful of believers led and sustained by prophetic guidance.

The worn-out farm taken over by Sutherland in 1904 through the guidance of Mother White became an agricultural wonder. The stones gathered from the rock-strewn acres became building material not only ready to the hand and without cost, but the builders found it suitable and sturdy. Even today some of the stonework of those early days endures. To renew the worn-out soil, Dr. Sutherland discovered that continual use of clover, cowpeas, and other leguminous crops built fertility. Turning under green crops, planting alfalfa, and following methods of intelligent farming produced a marvelous transformation. Edward Alexander Sutherland saw the Madison school farm become exactly what Mother White had predicted, "an object lesson to the Southern field."

Fruit raising developed into a major industry. Large peach, plum, and apple orchards flourished on the school property. Well-kept vineyards produced delicious grapes in abundance. A peach and apple orchard of more than three thousand trees grew at Ridgetop, Tennessee, on school land. They nourished the school and supplied the sanitarium. The whole population of the wide campus followed the motto, "We grow and can what we eat, and eat what we grow and can."

In one year the canning department put up a total of 3000 gallons of peaches, 1000 gallons of string beans, 2200 gallons of grapes, as well as lesser amounts of tomatoes, pears, and apples. Truly the farm produced abundantly.

Through this beautiful and lavish harvest the aging Dr. Sutherland often walked, hefting an enormous bunch of grapes or stroking a velvety peach, thumping a huge watermelon or exclaiming over the size and weight of a sweet potato from a wagonload of freshly dug tubers. At such time his heart swelled with wonder and gratitude, and he wished so much that Mother White could have seen all this richness and beauty. He thought also of his friend, Percy Magan, now growing old like himself but still full of faith and joy and the assurance that they had "not followed cunningly devised fables" back there in 1904; they had obeyed the prophetic guidance, which is more sure than the evidence of our senses.

One evening in 1940 Sally Sutherland spread some of the newspaper articles out on the table, and she and Edward stood looking at them.

"Does Percy have copies of all these?" Edward asked his wife.

"Yes, I think so." Sally leafed through them. "I just sent him the *Coronet* today. I knew he'd like to see your picture."

"The pictures are unimportant. The articles are unimportant except as they witness to the world that we have done God's will and He has blessed us." Edward looked at Sally. She was gray-haired and somewhat wrinkled now, but the same roguish smile still curved her lips and the same warm and merry heart animated her actions.

"You know we have been married almost fifty years," she reminded him.

"I have not forgotten." He smiled and laid his hand over hers.

On August 13 of that year the whole Madison campus joined in a celebration to commemorate the fiftieth anniversary of Dr. and Mrs. Sutherland's marriage. Dr. P. P. Claxton, president of Austin Peay Normal School; H. K. Christman, circulation manager of the Southern Publishing Association; and Cecil Sims of the law firm, Bas, Berry and Sims paid sincere tribute to the honored pair and recalled highlights of their long years of service. The celebration ended when Dr. and Mrs. Sutherland drove away in a horse and buggy while their well-wishers sang, "Put On Your Old Gray Bonnet."

Dr. Sutherland looked upon all the public acclaim and its resultant interest as the direct fulfillment of the prophecies Mother White had made about the project back in 1904. He took every opportunity to tell visitors and those with whom he came in contact of the Lord's leading and guiding hand.

The farm had suffered its times of adversity. Sutherland remembered vividly the freeze back in March 1921 that had ruined the fruit crop, and another year a severe hailstorm had destroyed the gardens and much of the fruit; but now, in 1943, Madison farm suffered its most serious and prolonged natural adversity. A drought began in May and lasted for eighty days. Not a drop of rain fell. Everything dried up.

The Madison family turned to God for help. On the afternoon of Sabbath, July 24, they met in the chapel and entreated the Lord for rain. The following morning the sun, a flaming disk, spread its ruinous heat as it had for so many days. By noon the blistering heat scorched the parched land with pitiless intensity.

That evening Dr. Sutherland gathered everyone into the chapel. "We will praise God for the rain He is going to send." He smiled at them as they filed in and took their places. Tears mingled with the songs of praise. The Spirit of God seemed to fill the assembly. Different ones began moving about the room making wrongs right and renewing friendships under the powerful impetus of the Spirit. After two hours, everyone went home. Most of them went rejoicing, but a few doubted that Dr. Sutherland's prayers would prevail with the Lord. These discussed the dire fate of Madison if no rain should come. "What would people think about these Christians who prayed for rain without results?" They shook their heads and decided to "wait and see."

Monday morning brought no relief. The sun rose clear and bright as the day before. Whispers flew round the wilted gardens and the close, hot rooms. Now what? Dr. Sutherland's relationship with his God stood challenged. But, like Elijah on Mount Carmel, the doctor's faith held firm, and the majority stood with him. The school family assembled for their noon meal, and afterward small groups of students sat around discussing the fearful idea of unanswered prayer.

By midafternoon clouds began to gather. Dr. Sutherland sent out word for all the farm workers to gather in from the fields. He urged all workers, students and faculty, to gather in the chapel at once, for the rain would be upon them. They all hurried in while rain began to pelt down from a black and heavy sky. No thunder shower, this; the rain continued to pour. It fell all though the evening and well into the night.

Before Dr. Sutherland went to bed, he opened the window of the bedroom and let the blessed downpour blow into the room while he and Sally stood hand in hand thanking God.

"Did you see the rainbow this afternoon?" Sally asked.

"Yes, right in the middle of the storm. Never saw a more perfect one." Then Edward Alexander Sutherland repeated the promise he had claimed; "I will give you the rain of your land in his due season, the first rain and the latter rain, that thou mayest gather in thy corn, and thy wine, and thy oil. And I will send grass in thy fields for thy cattle."

About noon the following day rumors began to reach the campus that the rain had not been general, but had fallen only on the Neely Bend section —a small area—but this area included all of the Madison farm! Not till ten days later did a general rain relieve the stricken earth.

One morning Dr. Sutherland told Sally that some fifty students from Scarritt College would be spending the day at Madison.

"Who are they?" Sally looked up from her sewing. "Some special group?" she asked.

"They are all missionaries attending the short summer course the college gives for missionaries under appointment and for those returning after furlough. Since a lot of them are headed for Japan, I've told Perry Webber to show them around."

"You will see them too, won't you?" Sally asked.

"Of course. I always enjoy telling them how

Mother White got guidance direct from heaven about this place." He started for the door. "I want everyone to know that we didn't do this ourselves. We had divine direction and assistance."

Dr. Perry Webber guided the large group of visitors around the campus, outlining Madison's fundamental principles of education. He showed them both sanitarium and college and explained how the two institutions supported one another. At noon they were served a delicious luncheon consisting of products from the health food factory.

One missionary on furlough from India spoke the opinion of many: "This sort of thing is just what we need to build character in India. We need to train men and women who can care for themselves; can stand on their own feet and train others to do the same."

Then Dr. Sutherland told them how the run-down farm had been purchased under the guidance and advice of Ellen G. White, who got her instructions from God Himself. He quoted her words: "The class of education given at the Madison School is such as will be accounted a treasure of great value by those who take up missionary work in foreign lands."

This entertaining of visitors now came to be a frequent happening on the campus. Distinguished visitors came from many lands to visit Madison. Marshall Feng Yu Hsiang, known to the world as "The Christian General," spent five days at Madison. Four high-ranking associates came with him, also Dr. Harry Miller, well known as the "China Doctor."

One day during their visit the general told Dr.

Sutherland, "I lived neighbor to a man in Nanking who came from Chao Tou Chen Training Institute, an institution patterned after Madison."

"That must have been Dr. Paul Quimby," Sutherland said.

"Yes, it was. Generalissimo and Madame Chiang Kai-Shek admired that school so much that they invited Dr. Quimby to be minister of education for the Sons and Daughters of the Revolution."

Dr. Sutherland's heart thrilled to know how far the influence of Madison had spread and with what glorious results. When Mother White had said that Ferguson Farm would become a strong center of training and influence, no human being could have visualized what growth and development were comprehended in that simple statement. Now Edward Alexander Sutherland walked home through the midst of the miracle, and in his heart he gave glory to God.

> "One good rule to keep in mind is that there are no crises with God, for no human problem can baffle His wisdom."—*Who Waits in Faith* by Harry Moyle Tippett, p. 12.

AT EVENING TIME—LIGHT

Madison School had entered the 1940s like a great ship under full sail with all flags flying. Edward Alexander Sutherland, still directing her course, saw troubled waters ahead.

In 1939 war had flamed in Europe, and Dr. Sutherland remembered the experiences of World War I. Madison had grown and expanded in the years between the two world wars, and all her progress and expansion had been of such a nature that the twin institutions were prepared to endure the restrictions imposed by war and its many hardships.

While Madison marched into the limelight of public favor and acclaim, the United States advanced into war against totalitarian imperialism.

Having walked with God through the first forty years of the twentieth century, Dr. Sutherland

11—G.B.F.

faced the changes of his old age with a strong faith and cheerful outlook. He still maintained his close friendship with Dr. Percy Magan; but now Percy's health had begun to fail, and in 1942 he resigned the position he had held for so many years as leader of the College of Medical Evangelists.

The year after World War II ended a change came about in Dr. Sutherland's relationship with the General Conference. For most of the years while he and his loyal associates struggled with the mighty problems at Madison, the organized church had stood on the sidelines and looked on without giving much help or encouragement. Often the leaders had been critical and sometimes even hostile. Now the leaders invited Edward Alexander Sutherland to come to the General Conference session of 1946 and report on his twin institutions and what God had done for them.

The church leaders had noted the worldwide publicity through the *Reader's Digest* article and other magazines and newspapers. The work at Madison, planted under the direct counsel of Ellen White and carried forward according to divine direction, could no longer be ignored. Half a hundred smaller replicas of Madison were functioning all through the Southern States, and the influence of Sutherland and his work had spread around the world. Also Dr. Sutherland held the respect and admiration of most of the church membership. The urge for more self-supporting institutions could not be denied or set aside. Dr. Sutherland went to the General Conference. And God went with him. He told his story, and God's Spirit opened hearts to comprehend and receive it.

When Edward Alexander Sutherland stood before the General Conference in that 1946 session, he had been president of Madison College for over forty years. He had been thirty-nine years old when he and Percy Magan together with Mother White and the others had founded the Madison School in the bend of the Cumberland River on the rocky, barren acres of Ferguson Farm.

The General Conference, at this 1946 session, set up the North American Commission of Self-Supporting workers and made Dr. Sutherland president of the new commission. By so doing they took notice of the expanding influence of the self-supporting work. Also they set forth clearly before the whole denomination what Sutherland and Magan had done by total devotion to the principles of education as set forth by Ellen G. White.

The following spring, in March of 1947, representatives of self-supporting institutions run by Seventh-day Adventists met in Cincinnati, Ohio, and they organized the Association of Seventh-day Adventist Self-supporting Institutions. Edward Alexander Sutherland had celebrated his eighty-second birthday on March 3. The organizational session convened on March 4 and 5. Probably no birthday remembrance throughout his life matched this one for joy and satisfaction. He talked it over with Sally.

"Do you suppose we can send Percy a complete report of what has happened?"

Sally lifted tired eyes, and her husband noted that the laughter wrinkles still beautified her sweet face. "I think Percy may not be able to read letters anymore. He has been ill so long."

In December of that same year Percy Magan died, and the heart of his loyal friend ached with a great longing to see Percy and tell him all about the newest developments in the self-supporting work and the new and belated vindication of all their faith and all their struggles through the General Conference action. Now he must wait until the resurrection morning.

Dr. Sutherland, on that December day in 1947, walked through the miracle that Madison had become. He saw in it a foretaste of what beauties will be seen in the earth made new, when he and Percy would view it together. True, he realized that nothing could fully reveal to him now the full glory of "God's Beautiful Farm" as it would appear with everlasting life springing up in every bud and blossom; but he did see it with an extended vision, and those who loved him marked the look in his blue eyes, that prophetic look that revealed the vision of God's glorious purpose unfolding in days to come.

Dr. Sutherland's new responsibilities in the Association of Self-supporting Institutions took him to church headquartes in Washington, D. C., often and kept him there for varying periods of time. He could not take Sally with him, for she had become too frail.

The couple often talked of the joyful celebration Madison would have on its fiftieth anniversary in 1954, but Sally did not live to take part in the festivities. She fell asleep in 1952. The evening shadows had begun to lengthen around the heroic old pioneer. Percy had been laid to rest five years earlier, and now his Sally! As he stood by her casket and gazed into the beloved face, the comfort of God enfolded him. His face, which for over half a century had "been set like a flint Zionward," took on new lines of hope and determination. He looked on his children, Dr. Joe and Yolanda, and knew how blessed he had been to have had such a woman as Sally as a companion and the mother of his son and daughter.

Madison and all it stood for became even dearer after Sally's death.

"What hath God wrought!"—S. F. B.
Morse

AFTER FIFTY YEARS

As the fiftieth year of Madison's life unfolded,
Dr. Sutherland looked back. Mother White had
been laid to rest thirty-nine years ago. Percy
Magan had left Madison to foster the College of
Medical Evangelists in Loma Linda, California;
and he had passed away over six years ago. Sally
too had been laid to rest. Of the pioneers only two
yet remained—Edward Alexander Sutherland and
M. Bessie DeGraw.

In 1954, the golden anniversary year, the farm
covered 721 acres with a ridgetop farm of 91 acres.
The school also had the use of 100 acres lying
south of Neely Bend Road and owned by the
Layman Foundation.

Hundreds of people visited Madison campus
every year, attracted by its flowers, trees, and the
general loveliness of the spot. Groups of women

166

representing garden clubs of Nashville and other communities followed Dr. Floyd Bralliar and Richard Walker about the campus while the two botanists named the plants and described their native habitat and imparted interesting bits of nature lore.

A cedar of Lebanon stood at either side of the east entrance to the administration building. Not far away grew specimens of the only other true cedars in existence, the Atlantic cedar and the deodar.

Shrubs with delicate lavender blossoms perfumed the air around the east door. From their crushed wood and seeds frankincense is made. Bristle-toothed oaks from China grew here, and in season sixty flowering Japanese cherries in full blossom called forth exclamations of admiration from the visitors. Dr. Bralliar had brought these and many other exotic plants and flowers to the campus. Madison had become like a garden of Eden.

God, in His infinite mercy and wisdom, looked down on our lost and perplexed planet during the twentieth century of its whirl through time and space and set a series of miraculous events in motion. As in all God's plans, He had already chosen the men and the place for this mighty happening. He brought Edward Alexander Sutherland and Percy T. Magan together, gave them the experience they needed while they were still young and impressionable, and led them through severe discipline and great tests of faith. Then He brought them to the Ferguson Farm on the green banks of the Cumberland, and there He began a miracle so remarkable that even today its effects are felt in the far corners of the earth.

God accomplished this wonderful thing because He found a handful of men and women who believed in Him from the depth of their natures. Also they believed His messenger, and through them He worked His wonders. They had, in their youth, accepted the message of righteousness by faith and yielded their lives to the control of God's Holy Spirit. They were as human as all the rest of us, but their trust in God reached sublime heights and took hold of divine power. Now, on the fiftieth anniversary of Madison's life, many backward looks fortified that faith and strengthened confidence in what God would do in the years to come.

Although only two of the original pioneers still remained, many others had given many years of their lives to building Madison and in fostering its ideals. And the "units," little replicas of Madison, had sprung up throughout the southland. In many of these "units" schools joined with sanitariums for a balanced ministry. No one knows the countless blessings they have provided. Their record is written in heaven.

The golden anniversary year saw the sanitarium expanded to a 220-bed facility and fully staffed with qualified physicians and nurses. During the half century of Madison's history, she had sent out five hundred graduate nurses who now served in many places. One thousand alumni had gone out from Madison School to bless the world. The influence of Madison spread throughout the world and permeated the educational and medical work of the Seventh-day Adventist Church like yeast.

The twin institutions stood in the center of the huge farm, which produced abundant supplies of food and provided a spacious campus for the many attractive buildings. Many of them had been built with native stone gathered from the property. The students and their instructors used unique artistry and skill which still provided, in this anniversary year, enduring proof that solid and lasting structures had been erected here.

A modern food factory produced a wide variety of delicious health foods that were shipped all over the United States and also to foreign countries.

A family of 125 workers lived on the campus and carried on all the activities connected with the school, sanitarium, farm, and the many industries. Two apartment houses and eleven cabins had been provided for workers, while forty-three private homes belonged to the institution.

Looking back over half a century of progress, Dr. Edward Sutherland could see how God had blessed, not only with the material prosperity of good crops, full college enrollment, and full patient occupancy at the sanitarium; not only in the wide distribution of Madison health foods, and in the success of student enterprises whether on campus or in the "units"—God's blessings also appeared in the spiritual tone of the whole complex institution, the type of fellowship they enjoyed, the kindness they showed each other in sharing all good things. "The blessing of the Lord, it maketh rich, and he addeth no sorrow with it." Proverbs 10:22.

The two of the "rainbow seven" pioneers remaining on the campus blessed the place with their wise and loving counsel, their unfailing good judgment and common sense—Dr. Sutherland and Miss M. Bessie DeGraw. Since Sally Suther-

Two of the "rainbow seven" pioneers, Edward Sutherland and Bessie DeGraw, after more than 50 years of working together, united their lives in marriage.

land had passed to her rest in 1952, the days had been lonely for the aging doctor, and in April of the anniversary year (1954) a quiet wedding united these two remaining members of the "rainbow seven." They had worked together ever since Walla Walla College days and had teamed up with Percy Magan at Battle Creek College. They had helped move that college to Berrien Springs, Michigan, and suffered through four years of growing pains at that institution. They had pioneered the work at Madison with others of the "rainbow seven"; and now, in their sunset years, they decided to travel the remainder of their journey together. Dr. Sutherland was eighty-nine and his bride eighty-three.

As teacher and counselor, M. Bessie DeGraw had few peers. She had served as educational secretary for the Lake Union Conference. She had assisted both S. N. Haskell and Dr. Sutherland with important books. She had been editor of the *Advocate* from its first issue. In the early 1930s, when accreditation was being demanded of our educational institutions, she obtained her M.A. degree from Peabody College. At the age of sixty-one she completed with honors the course required for the Ph.D. degree. During the long period of years while she lived at Madison, she never failed to inspire the hearts and minds of her students with her own dedication and self-sacrifice.

Dr. Edward Alexander Sutherland had been president of the Madison School from 1904 to 1946. He had seen it develop under his guidance from a small, obscure school on a neglected farm to a fully accredited college recognized around the world and standing in a veritable Eden of gardens, orchards, and fields—so richly had God honored the simple faith of Madison's founders.

In 1946 Dr. Sutherland had been called to serve as secretary of the Association of Self-supporting Institutions and the Commission of Rural Living. Having put both these departments in order, he had returned to the Madison campus which he loved so much, intending to spend the remainder of his life surrounded by his many friends and helpers of the years gone by. Although in retirement, he counseled and guided in the affairs of Madison and many other self-supporting institutions.

In the golden year, celebrating a half-century of God's fulfillment of the plan He had revealed to Mother Ellen White so many years ago, no person rejoiced with more humble gratitude and sincere satisfaction than Dr. Sutherland. His eyes had always seen far beyond other people's vision. Now they took on the prophetic glow of his final years, as he viewed the distant reality of his beloved Madison as a promise of "God's beautiful farm"— in the earth made new.

"No man can lead others where he himself has not first gone. If a man wants to grow stronger, he must constantly be struggling with that which is beyond his own strength, that which requires the exercise of great faith."—A letter from Edward Alexander Sutherland to Percy Magan dated November 24, 1915.

PORTRAIT OF A HEROIC LEADER

For over a year after their marriage, the aged pair lived in their little white cottage on Madison campus, surrounded by those who knew and loved them and who cherished them for all the reasons that parents are cherished and for many more. Every person connected with the Madison institutions knew what the Sutherlands had done and why. They also knew who supplied the motivation and guidance for this miraculous work of faith.

Spring of 1955, in all its blossoming glory, had come again to the Cumberland. Flowers bloomed everywhere, and birds filled the air with sweet and continual melody. Edward Alexander Sutherland had reached his ninetieth year; and although he welcomed the flowers and sunshine as he always had, he felt a continual weariness. Now a distressing pain developed. His doctors advised him to spend a few days in the sanitarium, where the doctors diagnosed his ailment as appendicitis. A few days later, on June 20, 1955, he passed to his rest. His wife, Bessie DeGraw Sutherland, lived on for ten more years and quietly fell asleep on June 7, 1965, at the age of ninety-four.

When the word of Dr. Sutherland's death wafted across Madison campus, all activity came to a sudden halt as though a giant hand compelled all to stillness. Each person felt the shock in an intimate way, for Edward Alexander Sutherland had been many things to a multitude of people and a profound influence on all. Could it be possible? Had they taken for granted that he would always be with them? He had seemed indestructible, everlasting! And now he had gone!

The minds of thousands of people whose lives he had blessed turned now to contemplate what he had been to them, to Madison, to America, to the world. From the words they have spoken and written, this final portrait is painted. The palette is as wide as the world and the colors are varied and as vivid as the emotions of the human heart.

Edward Alexander Sutherland was a leader of men. He acquired by birth, by youthful dedication, and by constructive experience all the qualities that mark a heroic leader. Men followed him because they felt that he knew the way and that what lay at the end of the journey must be of infinite value. The fervor of his zeal compelled them.

He possessed a rare kind of courage that persisted in marching toward the goal no matter what obstacles lay ahead or what forces combined to obstruct his plans. This superb courage came from no reckless foolhardiness. Edward Alexander Sutherland knew the hand of God upon him, the light of God around him; and he had a deep respect for the "recompense of reward" that his Lord had promised. This aspect of his courage enabled him for so many years to bear without bitterness or resentment the hostility of those who should have supported and assisted him.

In the days of his youth, before the Madison experience, he and his associates established two important colleges that stand today as successful centers of learning for Christian youth—Walla Walla College and Emmanuel Missionary College (now a part of Andrews University). Then God led him, with Percy Magan, to the Cumberland and the stony, neglected farm that would become the site of Madison School and Madison Sanitarium. For fifty years he guided the affairs of Madison into such fruitfulness that it became, as Mother White had predicted, "a spectacle to the world, to angels, and to men."

Dr. Sutherland was a father, not only to his own son, Joe, and his daughter, Yolanda, but to thousands of other young people who sat under his teaching and felt the magic of his outgoing affection.

"He taught me how valuable I was to God and made me understand the worth of my own soul," one student said.

Love, compassion, and wisdom enabled this man to be a good neighbor. He understood the needs of the poor and deprived, and he devised methods for lifting them up into God's plan for successful living in this world as well as in the world to come. Thousands of men and women around the world are serving humanity because of the influence Edward Alexander Sutherland shed about on all who associated with him.

Perhaps he will be best remembered as an educator, for he devoted his long life to understanding "the true science of education." He, more than any other person, fostered the early schools for the children of the church. He is rightly regarded as the father of Seventh-day Adventist church schools. He wrote textbooks for them; he planned their curriculums; he carried them on his heart all his life. He got his blueprint from the Master Teacher Himself, and against all opposition he persisted in establishing about fifty of them in the Southern States. Because of Madison's example and influence many such centers of learning are in operation today all over the world. The full impact of this man's life and work can never be known until the heavenly records are opened to our wondering eyes.

Dr. Sutherland was an apostle of rural living. He understood God's purpose for the land, and he worked in harmony with divine principles to change the stony, worn-out Ferguson Farm into a little Garden of Eden. He demonstrated over and over again what God can do with humble and willing workers on a backwoods farm or a neglected acreage. He asked first, "Is it God's will?" Being assured that God's will required it, he bent every energy of his complex nature to do God's will in the fastest and most efficient way. For every success he gave God the glory and the praise. To the end of his life he remained a humble and unassuming person.

Dr. Sutherland is also remembered as a healer,

for he followed the Great Healer in paths of compassion and service. He ministered to the heartsick, the discouraged, and the weak in faith. Later, he became a healer of men's bodies through his work as a trained physician. He led out in medical institutions. His wisdom comprehended their needs and their priorities. He could and did plan ahead for their development along balanced lines of efficiency. His vision reached even to foreign lands, and he foresaw what could be accomplished with God's methods.

As a college president, a doctor, a father, a citizen, a neighbor, or a friend he witnessed for his Lord. He lived, worked, and planned with the same objective that motivated his Master's life— "He lived to bless others." To him, Christianity meant walking with God each day and in every relationship of life.

From the early years of his ministry as an educator, Dr. Sutherland advocated rural living; and the passing years only strengthened his conviction that everyone should live in the country and support himself and his family from the land and the labor of his own hands. The "units" sprang up around Madison through the years and demonstrated how God would bless the efforts of plain people when they obeyed His will and followed His blueprint. To foster establishment of the "units" and maintain them, he helped organize the Layman Foundation and persevered until he saw the work of self-supporting institutions received into the organized structure of the church as the Association of Seventh-day Adventist Self-supporting Institutions.

Along the California coast grows a magnificent

tree known as the coast redwood. It propagates itself through shoots that spring up around the trunk of the parent tree, thus producing a "redwood circle."

Through just such a miraculous process—new growth—the "units" in the Southern States, together with health and educational centers all over the world, stand as lively witnesses to the enduring inspiration of Madison. They are the memorial to a man whom God used to accomplish one of His greatest works on planet Earth—Edward Alexander Sutherland.

EPILOGUE

Through the years since the golden anniversary celebration in 1954, the last member of the "rainbow seven" pioneers of Madison College was laid to rest, M. Bessie DeGraw Sutherland.

We are now in a period of transition as the vision and program of self-supporting work is passing through the opening portals into a new era. In the spirit of optimism, in the light of marvelous achievements, combined with an army of experienced, dedicated leadership, we envision the "Golden Cord" weaving its way through the remaining period of challenge and opportunity for the ultimate triumph of the vision of Christian education sponsored by E. A. Sutherland and his devoted associates.

The limitations of time and space necessitate a termination of this delineation of the life of Dr. E. A.

Sutherland in the Madison story. We have discovered that his philosohpy of Christian education and that of his associates at Madison College developed literally thousands of men and women of self-reliance and noble spirit who have made and are still making a significant contribution to the cause of God in many lines of endeavor.

During its maturing years Madison College cherished a burden to widen its sphere of influence by establishing community centers in the rural South dedicated to feature educational and health work. Teachers, workers, and students were anxious to do this type of work. However, capital funds were lacking, and it was difficult to become established except in a very meager way. The work progressed in a spirit of enthusiasm and sacrifice, and in due time centers appeared in places near to and far from the parent institution.

A number of these centers served as the nucleus for institutions which later became conference-operated units. Among these is Highland Academy (formerly Fountain Head School), which now serves as the boarding academy sponsored by the Kentucky-Tennessee Conference. Fountain Head School and Sanitarium was started by the Mulford and West families in 1907. This rural unit of Madison yielded not only an academy which is operated by the local conference, but also a hospital which is a member of the Southern Adventist Hospital System, the formal organization which coordinates the hospitals controlled and operated by the Southern Union Conference of Seventh-day Adventists.

The real story of the widening sphere of the Madison influence began when Mrs. Lida Funk

Scott arrived in Madison to seek rest and renewal of spirit after a great sorrow and disappointment had overtaken her. Her speedy recovery to normal health inspired in her a burden for spreading the Madison plan. Her personal visitation among community centers dedicated to educational and medical missionary work graced the great Southland and formed a pattern of collaboration in providing schools, nursing homes, sanitariums, hospitals, and training facilities for nurses, teachers, and agriculturalists. Many of the young people who have attended these centers have joined the graduates of Madison College in filling responsible positions in the United States and in foreign fields.

The original founders of the Layman Foundation have passed away; but the present board of trustees, under President Rodger F. Goodge, includes individuals who received their education and inspiration from the original founders of Madison College and similar units throughout the South.

It is for this reason that the Southern Union has a larger number of Seventh-day Adventist affiliated hospitals than any other union in the world. It is also largely because of the influence of Madison College that the Southern Union has more Seventh-day Adventists in its medical personnel than any other part of the world except the Pacific Union. The people in the Southern Union who leave it for medical training of various sorts almost invariably return to their southern homeland. It is undeniable that Madison College has had more to do with this than any other single factor in the history of the cause of God in the southeastern United States.

The early graduates of Madison College returned to their homes, and they constantly encouraged their followers to do so. A further rewarding feature of the Madison spirit is the prevailing emphasis upon proper and complete educational training. The Madison concept has been to encourage those who are capable of doing so to proceed as far educationally as they possibly can. Within the schools influenced by Madison College has been a determination to bring well-trained teachers into the ranks. Through the years in the various units encouragement has been given to intellectual attainment in every way possible without sacrificing moral and spiritual commitment which prompted the work. It is no secret that students who have come from self-supporting schools in the Southern Union have been some of the finest academicians which have presented themselves to Seventh-day Adventist colleges.

Probably no more heartening feature of the spirit of Madison was the firm insistence of its staff that they were not separate from God's work but, indeed, a part of it. Self-supporting work in the South did not begin because the founders of Madison or its satellites embarked upon ego trips or had an ax to grind as far as the Seventh-day Adventist Church was concerned. It is no secret, for example, that in our self-supporting schools there is a more conservative approach to life in general, and for this these schools are to be commended.

The prevailing concept of the founders of Madison College from the days of its inception was that their work was God's work—it was the work of the Seventh-day Adventist Church, God's church.

When they spoke about Madison as "our" school, they spoke of themselves and all other Adventists alike. The obligation of providing an education for God's people as a whole rested heavily upon their shoulders. Those pioneers had a single determination—that their college should serve all of God's people and that it should open the way for the program of God's work in the southeastern United States. The resounding success of the Southern Union rests squarely upon the foundation which our early Madison pioneers laid.

But all of the greatness of the Madison spirit and what it has produced in its schools throughout the United States is possible only because the leaders have sought out people for their institutions who are creative and bright and quick to observe, keen of judgment and unafraid of work. Self-supporting work in God's church demands people who are vigorous, not lazy; people who stimulate themselves mentally, not idle dreamers; people who have a vision, not daydreamers; people who distinguish between the voice of God and the whispering of temptation. Self-supporting work calls for people like that man identified in Jeremiah 17:8: "For he shall be as a tree planted by the waters, and that spreadeth out her roots by the river, and shall not see when he cometh, but her leaf shall be green; and shall not be careful of the year of drought, neither shall cease from yielding fruit."

And so the work of Madison continues in the ideals and lives of men and women who graced its halls and walked its campus. It is true that when shifting tides of educational endeavors and unstable economic situations forced the school into strait places, Madison College did not have a financial reserve to survive; and so the school was officially closed. But it has not really closed, because its work goes on forever in the hearts and ideals of those who were influenced. Its work lives in those people and their families and their children wherever they are, whatever they are doing. It is unfortunate when some people wistfully say, "Madison shall live again."

Madison does live. It has never died. Just as surely as God has honored the endeavors of that school and its people in the past, He will honor the conscientious labors of those who have been influenced by it and who continue God's work on this earth. Probably as no other school, Madison fulfills the counsel given by Peter, counsel which is both encouragement and a challenge: "As every man hath received the gift, even so minister the same one to another, as good stewards of the manifold grace of God." 1 Peter 4:10.

The Druillard Library at Madison, built from stone found on the farm.

Williams Hall, the girls' dormitory.

Gotzian Home, the boys' dormitory.

We'd love to have you download our catalog of
titles we publish at:

www.TEACHServices.com

or write or email us your thoughts,
reactions, or criticism about this
or any other book we publish at:

TEACH Services, Inc.
254 Donovan Road
Brushton, NY 12916

info@TEACHServices.com

or you may call us at:

518/358-3494

Produced in partnership with
LNFBooks.com